Twayne's Theatrical Arts Series

Warren French
EDITOR

Fritz Lang

Fritz Lang with Thea von Harbou

Fritz Lang

Robert A. Armour

Virginia Commonwealth University

BOSTON

Twayne Publishers

1977

Fritz Lang

is first published in 1978 by Twayne Publishers,
A Division of G. K. Hall & Co.

Copyright © 1978 by G. K. Hall & Co.

Printed on permanent/durable acid-free paper and bound
in the United States of America

First Printing, October 1978

Library of Congress Cataloging in Publication Data

Armour, Robert A
Fritz Lang.

(Twayne's theatrical arts series)
Bibliography: p. 177–79
Filmography: p. 180–96
Includes index.
1. Lang, Fritz, 1890–1976.
PN1998.A3L3556   791.43'0233'0924   78-6259
ISBN 0-8057-9259-7

Contents

About the Author

ROBERT ALEXANDER ARMOUR was born in Richmond, Virginia, on March 23, 1940. His B.A. came from Randolph-Macon College, his M.A. from Vanderbilt University, and his Ph.D. from the University of Georgia (1968). He is now an associate professor in the English Department of Virginia Commonwealth University in Richmond. Even though he teaches a variety of literature and composition courses, his special interest has been film for a number of years. He teaches Fiction into Film in the English Department and Film as a Teaching Medium for the School of Education. On two occasions he has been awarded NEA grants for training high-school and elementary film teachers. He has published articles on film in the *English Journal*, the *Journal of the University Film Association*, and the *Literature/Film Quarterly;* and he has written the chapter on film bibliography for the forthcoming *Handbook of Popular Culture*. His continuing interest is in the relationship between poetry and film.

Editor's Preface

THE CLAIMS of Fritz Lang to a place in a series of books on outstanding contributors to the theatrical arts are beyond dispute. Andrew Sarris in *The American Cinema* places Lang among fourteen "pantheon directors," the supreme exemplars of their art; and, though critics might debate his exact placement in relationship to Chaplin, Griffith, and Welles and fellow Germans Lubitsch, Murnau, and von Sternberg, all would be likely to concede that for the four decades between the first and the final Dr. Mabuse films, Lang played an enormous role in shaping two national cinemas, each experiencing one of its greatest periods—the silent era of the German Weimar Republic and the American "studio years" of the 1930s and 1940s.

Lang's influence on younger directors has also been unparalleled. Jean-Luc Godard paid direct tribute in *Contempt* to the older director's influence on the development of the French New Wave—Lang himself appears in the film, majestically isolated from the world writhing below him, stoically contemplating its follies. The indirect influences of his fantastic and Expressionistic German films have manifested themselves from Douglas Fairbanks's *The Thief of Bagdad* to Steven Spielberg's *Close Encounters of the Third Kind*, while Lang's bold interjection in *Fury* and *You Only Live Once* of outraged social commentary into the often timorous American film of the Depression years opened the way for the later production of such once unthinkable pictures as *Gentlemen's Agreement*, *The Defiant Ones*, *The Man with the Golden Arm*, and *The Boys in the Band*.

Lang's career has already been studied extensively, especially by his longtime friend Lotte Eisner. Instead of simply reviewing earlier tributes, however, Robert Armour has contributed to this series a fresh account of Lang that is distinctive on two counts. First, instead of simply reviewing Lang's career picture by picture, Armour provides a framework for a comprehensive appraisal of Lang's achievement by concentrating upon the director's particular concern throughout his work with what Nicholas Barlett has described as "the dark struggle," the endless warfare between the tendencies toward good and evil in man's nature—a subject painfully closely related to Lang's own perceptions of two World Wars and the rise of German Nazism as a threat to the civilized world. (As Andrew Sarris points out, "Lang's prevailing image is that of a world ravaged and in flames.") Although Lang never filmed his own version of Robert Louis Stevenson's frequently adapted novel *Dr. Jekyll and Mr. Hyde,* Armour points out that its allegory of man's dual nature is "the central motif" in Lang's work.

Second, although much of the criticism of Lang has justifiably concentrated upon his remarkable achievements in making German cinema perhaps the world leader during the great years of the silent films in the 1920s, Armour, after an initial appraisal of the importance to Lang's career of two of his largest undertakings, the Nibelungen films in the 1920s, Armour, after an initial appraisal of the importance to Lang's career of two of his largest undertakings, the Nibelungen which he dramatized manifestations of new forms of the "dark struggle" during years of increasing violence and paranoia in American life. Perhaps less outstanding than his German silents and his two earliest American films, these later films—as Armour points out—constitute a coherent group of increasingly dark and pessimistic statements about life in his adopted country. These films provide a rich and largely unstudied insight into the adaptation of a talented, established artist's response to a new situation and of the reflection in this work of the mounting tensions and frustrations of a period during which a once too naive people came to realize that even the achievement of the unconditional surrender of an enemy and the development of a superweapon capable of destroying a terrified world could not bring about tranquility and the desired release from further responsibility for controlling man's evil nature.

Although some critics have been put off by the heavy-handed symbolism at the end of Lang's *Metropolis,* his Manichean vision has perhaps never been more climactically crystallized than in that moment when the ultimate point is made that the head and hand cannot work together harmoniously without the mediation of the heart. Obvious as this concept may be, it never becomes banal because it has never been displaced or refuted. Man remains a victim of the "dark struggle" so long as he is trapped between the machinations of the greedy intellect and the unchecked power of the thoughtless body. Skillful as he was in the development of technological devices, Lang never allowed his films to be merely formal exercises indulging his virtuosity. He remained a determined moralist, dedicated to a vision of a world free from the self-aggrandizing destructiveness of the Dr. Mabuses in their dark holes, a world in which man's sacred human dignity might flourish at last in the sunlight. Indeed, as Armour points out, Lang in an interview spoke of the film director as "a kind of psychoanalyst." He remains unchallenged as one of the first to devote great gifts to the realization of an ancient and timeless vision in the distinctive medium of an unprecedented technological age that has posed hitherto unimagined threats of dehumanization.

WARREN FRENCH

Preface

THE ONLY MOVIE I can remember seeing twice when I was a boy was *An American Guerrilla in the Philippines*. At the time I was ten and fascinated by the tough yet kind Americans who were able to hold off the Japanese hordes until MacArthur returned. Like most boys of the early fifties, I went to many cowboy and war movies, but images from this one stuck in my mind at an age when I was most impressionable. I certainly had no theoretical thoughts about the effect of the film on my attitudes toward war, and I do not remember when I first knew that Fritz Lang made the movie. Nor do I remember when I first realized that it is not a very good movie.

But I do remember sitting in the Library of Congress while working on this book and rewatching the movie after a lapse of twenty-seven years. Many of the images were as fresh to me as they had been the first time I had seen the film, but suddenly I had insights into the way those images had influenced my boyish mind. During the early sixties I had been slow to accept the fact that America was losing the war in Viet Nam; but as I watched this film in a corner of our governmental library, I understood why I had been reluctant to believe what I read in the newspapers and saw on television about Viet Nam. Fritz Lang had told me that Americans were the best guerrilla fighters in the world; Tyrone Power had been human but invincible. Not only that, but it had been the clear responsibility of the Americans to liberate the Filipinos from their oppressors. What I had learned in 1950 at the Henrico Theater in Highland Springs, Virginia, had so impressed me that it took the words of many courageous Americans and the deaths of even more courageous men on both sides to convince me that Americans were not very good jungle fighters and had no business in the war anyway.

Such is the power of film, such is the power of myth, and such is the power of Fritz Lang to use his medium. As a recorder of humankind's myths and a depictor of archetypes, Lang's films have become for many viewers an expression of our eternal struggle against the forces trying to deprive us of our humanity. Those forces represent evil whatever form they take—enemy soldier, mechanical robot, sinister killer, or simply the corrupt side of human nature. Lang's vision of humanity is that we are constantly in a struggle which may overwhelm us, may defeat us, may force us to discover our strengths, may ennoble us, but will most assuredly change us. This book will concentrate on the struggles—both interior and exterior—in the films of Fritz Lang.

There are certain limitations on the scope of this study of Lang's films. The concentration will be on the theme of the dark struggle within his characters; the book is not an analysis of all of his films. Lotte Eisner has given a complete analysis of Lang's entire canon in her book. This book, on the other hand, is a study of only one of his major themes. The book is also limited by the fact that it is part of a series to be published by the same publisher. One of the other books in the series will concentrate on German Expressionism and will feature *Metropolis*; this study of Lang's films, therefore, recognizes the importance of Expressionism in shaping Lang's style and outlook and of *Metropolis* but does not feature either the movement or the film.

The reader should be cautioned that the prints of Lang's films appear in various conditions around the world. Some effort is being made to restore a few of his films to their original condition, as Blackhawk Films did with their recent release of *Siegfried* (but even this fine print is missing two important sequences). The two feature-length parts of the first Dr. Mabuse film have been combined into a much shorter single film. The only print I have been able to see of *The Return of Frank James* is in black and white, missing the color that impressed several of its contemporary reviewers. And Eisner says that the print of *M* from which she worked, presumably at the Cinémathèque Française in Paris, is missing a shot of the three mothers sitting outside the courtroom in the final scene. This shot does appear in American prints I have seen. The viewer can never be sure that he or she is seeing the film exactly as Lang left it or as other viewers see it.

I wish to thank the following persons for their help in the preparation of this book: Barbara J. Humphrys at the Library of Congress and Mary Corliss at the Museum of Modern Art, Wilnette Dyer and her crew at audio-visual at Virginia Commonwealth University, and my typists: Shannon Hughes, Bonnie Boone, and Susan Woolford. Appreciation must also be expressed to colleagues who offered advice and criticism: Elizabeth Reynolds, Walter Coppedge, Steve Segal, and John Noonan and his staff. Special thanks must go to Lawrence Laban for reading the entire manuscript and to Rosemary VanLandingham for her help with the frame enlargements. The stills have been provided by Glenn Photo Supply and the Museum of Modern Art.

Chronology

1890   Fritz Lang born in Vienna, Austria, December 5.

1908– Studies architecture at the Academy of Graphic Arts in Vi-
1910   enna. Leaves home and begins to study art.

1913   Moves to Paris and begins career as artist.

1914   When war breaks out, he returns to Vienna, enters the army, and is wounded.

1918   While recuperating he plays a role in a local play and is noticed by someone in the German film industry who suggests that he come to Berlin to work in the movies.

1919   Goes to Berlin and begins writing scrips for both Decla and UFA, the leading studios in Germany at the time. Occasionally he acts in minor roles in the films; directs his first film, *Halb-Blut*, also *Der Herr Der Liebe*, and *Die Spinnen*; scheduled to work on *The Cabinet of Dr. Caligari* but *Die Spinnen* is so successful he is asked to make a second part; *Hara-Kiri*.

1920   *Die Spinnen*, part two; *Das Wandernde Bild*; working for the first time with Thea von Harbou; *Vier Um Die Frau*.

1921   Marries his second wife, Thea von Harbou. (Little is known of his first wife); *Der Müde Tod*—Douglas Fairbanks buys the American rights and withholds release until he can borrow the special effects and use them in *Thief of Bagdad*.

1922   *Dr. Mabuse, Der Spieler*, in two parts.

1924   *Die Nibelungen*, in two parts. Spends two years on production of this film.

1927   *Metropolis*.

1928   *Spione*.

1929   *Frau Im Mond*.

1931   *M*, his first sound film.

1933   *Das Testament des Dr. Mabuse*, his second film on Mabuse and his last in Nazi Germany; afraid of the Nazis' discovering his Jewish background, he leaves Germany in a hurry. He leaves behind his money, his citizenship, and his wife. *Liliom*, in Paris.

1934   Goes to Hollywood to work for MGM but spends many months on unrealized projects. He travels and learns English.

1936   *Fury*, his first American film.

1937   *You Only Live Once*.

1938   *You and Me*.

1940   *The Return of Frank James*, his first color film.

1941   *Western Union; Man Hunt*.

1943   *Hangmen Also Die!* Works with fellow German Bertolt Brecht on the script.

1944   *Ministry of Fear; The Woman in the Window*.

1945   *Scarlet Street*.

1946   *Cloak and Dagger*.

1948   *Secret beyond the Door*.

1950   *House by the River; An American Guerrilla in the Philippines*.

1952   *Rancho Notorious*, with fellow German Marlene Dietrich; *Clash by Night*.

1953   *The Blue Gardenia; The Big Heat*.

1954   *Human Desire*.

1955   *Moonfleet*.

1956   *Beyond a Reasonable Doubt*.

1959   *Der Tiger von Eschnapur*, made in India for a German production company, based on a story originally written by Lang and von Harbou in 1920.

1960   *Die Tausend Augen des Dr. Mabuse*, his last film.

1963   Acts in *Le Mepris (Contempt)* for Jean-Luc Godard.

1976   Dies in home in Beverly Hills, California, August 2, after spending his last years there.

1

An Overview of the Life and Career of Fritz Lang

AS HE GREW OLDER Fritz Lang began to refer to himself as the "Last of the Dinosaurs";[1] this ironic description seems well fitted as a metaphor for the life and career of one of our greatest filmmakers. Like the dinosaur, Lang's image dominates the world around him; and like the dinosaur he became something of an anachronism in his own time—a man who had retained the values of an earlier age but who had achieved remarkable artistic expression of those values.

Even though he is thought of as German and American, he was actually born an Austrian, in Vienna on December 5, 1890. His mother's name was Paula, his father's, Anton. His father was a municipal architect and desired his son to follow that profession. Fritz had other visions of his future, but to make peace he agreed to attend lectures in engineering at the Technische Hochschule. Those studies were soon neglected for painting. Despite the early rejection of architecture and engineering as careers, the visual aspects of those disciplines continued to influence the career he did choose. He remained fascinated by buildings and found ingenious ways to blend them into his motion pictures, often making them an integral part of his theme or symbolism. He took an active interest in the construction of the sets for his films. The results of the influence of architecture and engineering are memorable: the gigantic wall in *Destiny,* the futuristic city in *Metropolis,* the cathedral steps in *Siegfried,* the prison cell in *You Only Live Once,* among others.

According to Lang's autobiography, other influences that he felt as a young man that later were reflected in his film career were his reading and his love of the theater. But it was painting that became his first love (a strong argument could be made that his first love was for women, but analyzing their influence on his career is a dangerous practice of which only the most unwary would not steer clear). To avoid continuing arguments with his father, Lang left home and

17

Lang working in Germany

began to wander—to Africa, Asia Minor, even the south Pacific. Finally he landed in Paris in the glamorous days before World War I and began to earn his keep selling his hand-painted post cards and newspaper cartoons. He continued to study painting, but in his spare time he went to the movie theater to watch the early examples of what he slowly realized was a new art form.

But then in August, 1914, war broke out; and as an Austrian in enemy territory, Lang was detained by the French police. He quickly escaped and caught the last train back to Vienna. There he rented a studio and began to set up as an artist, but did not make much progress before being called into the army. The details of his military service are a bit muddled now, but this much is certain: he rose to officer rank, was wounded more than once, and was decorated more than once. His wounds were serious: one led to the loss of sight in his right eye. During the months he spent in the military hospital, he began to write screenplays and sold two to the well-known German filmmaker Joe May. Then in 1918 he was declared unfit for further front-line duty and was sent to a hospital in Vienna to recuperate. While there, sitting one day in a sidewalk café, he was offered a role in a stage play; needing money, he accepted. At one of the performances, he attracted the notice of people from the German movie industry; and they suggested that he come to Berlin and work for Decla, the leading studio. Decla was headed by Erich Pommer, the man Lang says spotted him in the play and extended the invitation.

In August, 1918, he moved to Berlin and began to write screenplays and occasionally to act in minor roles in the studio's productions. Pommer's confidence in him rose quickly and by early 1919 he was directing his first film, *The Half Breed*, to be released early in April of that year. For several months he combined the roles of acting, scriptwriting, and directing; the most notable of the films he directed at this time were *The Spiders* (1919), a complicated and lengthy story about a search for Inca treasure, and *Hara-Kiri* (1919), an adaptation of *Madame Butterfly*. The success of these films led to additional directing assignments.

During this period he began to collaborate with a young woman screenwriter named Thea von Harbou. Once they established a working relationship the two worked on all the films Lang was to make until he left Germany in the early thirties. Lang divorced his first wife and married von Harbou. She was to be given writing

Destiny: Death before the wall

credits for the films and he, the directing credits; but it is clear that they together wrote all the screenplays. The true story of their collaboration probably will not be known. The extent to which she influenced his choice of plots, his tendency toward sentimentality, or his politics cannot be determined. With collaboration as personal and extensive as theirs, their mutual influences must have been complicated. When he left Germany, she remained and joined the Nazi party.

For a while it seemed that he would get a chance to direct *The Cabinet of Dr. Caligari,* and he spent some time working on the project. It was he that suggested the frame story that was to place the narrator of the strange adventures of Dr. Caligari and Caesar as an inmate in an insane asylum. The popularity of *The Spiders,* however, led the studio to decide to have Lang direct a second part and assign *Caligari* to Robert Wiene.

Lang's first major film was *Destiny* (1921). This allegorical tale concerns the efforts of a young woman to bargain with death for the life of her boyfriend. Death, a figure similar to that of Death in Bergman's *The Seventh Seal,* gives her three chances to save a human life. Three times—first in Arabia, then Quattrocento France, and finally at the court of the emperor of China—she fails. Lang's use of special effects here almost overpowers the narrative of the story. He used special costumes, elaborate set design that borders on parody of Expressionism, and a flying carpet. Death, however, offers her one more chance to save her friend. If she can produce a life to exchange for the man's, Death will set him free. She tries to convince several people to sacrifice themselves for her lover but is unsuccessful. Finally in a fire she has the option of rescuing or sacrificing a baby. Death is standing beside her, waiting for her decision. She pauses, then hands the baby through the window to its mother and safety. The woman then gives herself to Death and the two lovers are reunited in death. Lang's use of sets, lighting, and the theme of the power of fate are precursors of Lang's techniques and themes in his later films.

Destiny was followed by *Dr. Mabuse, the Gambler* (1922), the first of three films Lang was to make about this master criminal. With this film Lang begins to demonstrate the mastery of his technique and theme. He next went into the massive effort of turning the German myth of Siegfried and the Nibelungen treasure into a twentieth-century revenge story. The two films *Siegfried* and *Kriemhild's Revenge* (both 1924) as a unit are on the epic scale of their poetic source and show Lang's ability to direct a spectacle. With his next film he went into the future almost as far as he had gone into the past with the Nibelungen Saga. *Metropolis* (1926) deals with the struggles between the workers and management in a futuristic city, the scale of which is as grand as the forest of *Siegfried*. With these films Lang became one of the premiere filmmakers of Germany, and, for that matter, of the world.

In 1928 he directed *Spies*, a cloak-and-dagger story that uses a master criminal much like Dr. Mabuse. Then in 1929 he made his last silent film, *The Woman in the Moon*, a well-done tale of the future space exploration without the power of *Metropolis*.

Lang's first sound film was *M* (1931), the story of a murderer of children and the efforts of the police and professional criminals to capture him. All of Lang's films explore the psychological explanations for the characters' actions, but *M* becomes the prototype of films that enter into the mind of the murderer to study why he does as he does. Technically, the film shows that Lang was quick to master the use of sound.

As the Nazi party began to dominate politics in Germany, Lang returned to the theme of the master criminal and made his second film about Dr. Mabuse. *The Last Will of Dr. Mabuse* (1933) shows that Mabuse could dominate other criminals even from the insane asylum. The similarities between Mabuse and Hitler were not missed by the Nazis, and the film was suppressed.

The story of what happened next has been told often by Lang.[2] He was ordered to report to Dr. Goebbels, then German minister of propaganda. He dressed in striped trousers and cutaway coat and went, sure that he was on his way to official censure for his last film. Much to his surprise he was greeted warmly by Goebbels, who told him that Hitler was an admirer of Lang's films and wanted him to make films for the Third Reich. Lang, in a state of shock and positive that Goebbels did not know that Paula Lang was Jewish, was polite but sat there wondering if he could get to his bank and withdraw his money before it closed. Goebbels talked on and on and Lang missed the closing of the bank. He returned home, packed a few clothes, took what little jewelry he had about the house, and caught the next train to Paris. A little later the German tax people wrote him and requested that he return to discuss a tax problem. He never went back; sometime later he learned that his bank deposits had been confiscated.

He went to France and got a job making a film. *Liliom* (1934) was part tragedy and part comedy, the closest Lang came to making a comedy (several of his films contain nice comic touches, but a film that was completely comic would not have fit his philosophy of life).

Then he signed a contract with Metro-Goldwyn-Mayer and came to America in 1934. In the months that followed, Lang was unable to complete his contract with MGM to make a single picture as each of the scripts he prepared was rejected by David O. Selznick and the other officers of the studio. For about a year Lang spent some of his time working on a series of scripts that were never to be realized and traveling the rest of the time around America, learning about his adopted country. One of his first tasks was to learn English; he read and spoke only this new language, reading newspapers and comic strips from which he learned American humor and slang. During his travels he visited small towns and talked with ordinary people, gaining knowledge and insights that are probably reflected in his shift of focus from the heroic characters of the German films to the more ordinary ones of the American films.

The scripts that occupied Lang's professional time during these months came to very little. One, about a fire that had killed 125 people aboard the S.S. *Morro Castle* in the fall of 1934, was apparently too far ahead of its time. It seems to have been rejected because the studio was afraid it might offend the shipping companies. Today such a story would scarcely stand out among the rash of disaster stories being made into films, one of the best of which is *The Poseidon Adventure,* about a disaster aboard ship.

Finally MGM gave him the opportunity to make a film. On rather short notice he was given a script outline and told to begin work. The result was *Fury* (1936), the film many critics think to be his best American film. The film demonstrated that the affection he had shown in Germany for studying the psychological depths of his characters and for set design had not been lost, but he had discovered a simplicity of image and symbol that had been missing in his German films.

He followed *Fury* with two more films that illustrated his social awareness—*You Only Live Once* (1937) and *You and Me* (1938); but there is a major difference between them. *You Only Live Once* is the story of a former convict and his attempt to marry his girl and live a normal life. He fails to reenter society because the odds are against him, and the film ends in tragedy. Society has not given him a chance. *You and Me* picks up where *You Only Live Once* leaves off. It deals with a group of former convicts who have jobs and are also trying to succeed in the outside world. But after the opening scenes, the film loses its social bite and becomes a love story laced with comedy. The film never achieves the level of social importance of its predecessor. Lang's next assignments were for a pair of Westerns. *The Return of Frank James* (1940) and *Western Union* (1941) had ordinary Western scripts, but somehow Lang interjected his own world view and found ways to make them interesting and entertaining even though he was working under much studio pressure.

When World War II began, Lang turned his attention to his former oppressors. He made a series of anti-Nazi films that became part of Hollywood's war against the enemy. *Man Hunt* (1941), *Hangmen Also Die* (1943), *Ministry of Fear* (1944), and *Cloak and Dagger* (1946) all in one way or another deal with the Nazi threat to freedom. None is simply a war movie, inasmuch as all concentrate on the individual struggles of the participants.

Toward the end of the war and in the years immediately following, Lang turned to making movies that emphasized his early tendencies toward mystery and suspense. The films—*The Woman in the Window* (1944), *Scarlet Street* (1945), *Secret beyond the Door* (1948), and *House by the River* (1950)—deal with the psychological motivations for and impacts of crime.

Lang then returned to earlier subjects for his next two films. In *An American Guerrilla in the Philippines* (1950) he made another war film, but this time the enemy were the Japanese rather than the Nazis. The struggle, however, of the central character against the evil opponents remains the same. In *Rancho Notorious* (1952) Lang returned to the Western genre to make a strange film about the effect of the desire for revenge.

Then in the mid-fifties Lang directed a number of detective and criminal thrillers that emphasized, as always in his films, the theme of the struggle of good and evil. Lang never lost his desire to make a social comment in his films, and these films, made under the studio system, nevertheless reflect both his social awareness and his fascination with the way the human mind works. *Clash by Night* (1952), *The Blue Gardenia* (1953), *The Big Heat* (1953), *Human Desire*

(1954), *While the City Sleeps* (1956), and *Beyond a Reasonable Doubt* (1956) have similar themes and world views, but Lang had the ability even when working within a familiar genre to make each film distinctive. The only film of Lang's during this period that did not follow the generic pattern was *Moonfleet* (1955), which had a historical setting uncommon for the American Fritz Lang.

Lang had become increasingly dissatisfied with studio tampering with his films, and after *Beyond a Reasonable Doubt,* he decided not to make more movies in America. He was offered the opportunity by a German producer to go to India to make *The Tiger of Eschnapur* and its sequel *The Indian Tomb* both 1958). These films were based on a script Lang and von Harbou had written for Joe May during Lang's early days in Germany, but Lang had not been permitted to direct the first filmed version of the script.

Then in 1960 Lang returned to Germany to make what turned out to be his last movie, *The Thousand Eyes of Dr. Mabuse.* In this film he returns to one of his favorite themes, the work of the master criminal, which he modernizes by adding up-to-date technology as a weapon to be used by the criminal.

In 1963 Jean-Luc Godard convinced Lang to play a role in *Contempt,* a film about the making of movies. Lang plays a director by the name of Fritz Lang, and the film becomes a tribute to the career of a director who probably was better revered by the members of the French New Wave than by his German and American contemporaries.

Toward the end of his life Fritz Lang returned to the United States, where he lived in Beverly Hills, California. After a long illness he died there on August 2, 1976.

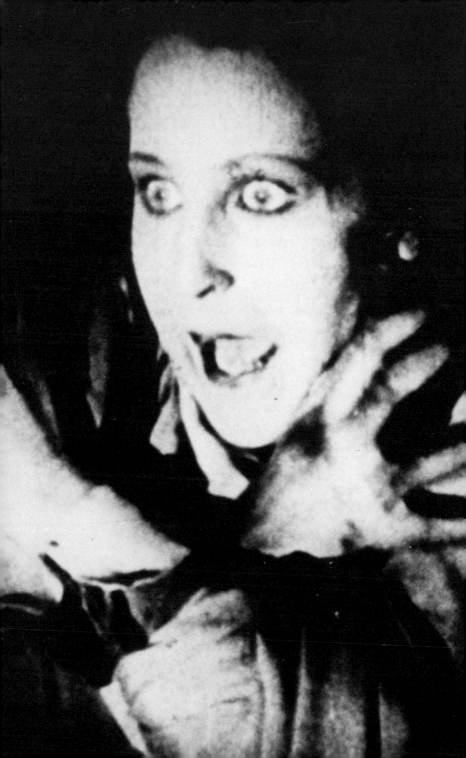

2

The Man Behind You: The Dark Struggle as Basic Theme

ONE OF THE UNREALIZED PROJECTS from Lang's early work in America contains elements of the central theme of his films. In 1935, he worked on a script called "The Man Behind You" and admitted that it was an expression of themes from earlier films: "It was a conglomerate of many things, many ideas I had had before—influenced by Jekyll and Hyde. My doctor is called Jyde. When the picture starts he is only interested in people, and he finds that there is in everyone a good being and an evil being."[1] The doctor goes insane over the love of an actress and discovers the evil within himself and his propensity for violence. The story of Jekyll and Hyde is well suited to explain the central motif in Lang's work. With uncanny faithfulness, Lang's films reflect the struggle within his people as they respond to the pushes and shoves from the dual sides of their character. In medieval morality plays the struggle would have been represented by good and bad angels whispering into the ear of the character trying to resolve his dilemma, and frequently Lang is able to find a similar material representation of the struggle.

Many of Lang's chief characters are people driven by some inner conflict of the sort symbolized by Jekyll and Hyde. Kriemhild, in Lang's version of *The Nibelungenlied*, is, at the opening of the film, a lovely woman; but after the murder of her husband, her loveliness is destroyed by her desire for revenge. She is willing to go to any lengths to satisfy her blood thirst, even if her brothers and former friends must suffer. She becomes an ugly woman, her face contorted by hatred. Her external fight is with her enemies, but it is her internal struggle over the conflict of loyalties that dominates the external struggle. In *Fury* Joe Wheeler is also consumed by the desire for revenge. He is willing to let the group of citizens go to their deaths for murder. He holes up in a dingy room and listens to

Metropolis: *Maria caught by Rotwang's light in the cave*

the progress of the trial over the radio. As the passion for revenge increases, he, like Kriemhild, shows his moral deterioration physically. He becomes an ugly, disheveled drunk. His girl friend, Katherine, breaks in on him and, after a fierce argument, tells him that everyone would have been better off if he had been killed in the fire for which he is seeking revenge. After a long walk he comes to understand what it is he is doing to himself and goes to the judge and confesses. And Dave Bannion in *The Big Heat* is also driven by revenge. After his wife is killed accidentally in a bomb explosion that was meant for him, Bannion allows a routine police case to turn into a personal vendetta. He, too, becomes corrupted by hatred for the criminals who destroyed his wife.

It should be clear that Lang's films do not exclusively dwell on these interior struggles, for such is not always the substance of exciting film entertainment. These interior struggles are triggered and symbolized by external struggles that bring visual excitement and suspense to the screen. The personal, inner struggles in Lang's films are the elements that give psychological realism to his characters, but the external struggles between the central characters and the forces that try to dominate them are the elements that motivate and give meaning to the inner struggles.

This inner struggle, what one London critic has quite appropriately called "The Dark Struggle,"[2] demonstrates that Lang is concerned with trying to understand man's psychological fears. Lang admitted to being a cinematic psychologist: "I consider a director a kind of psychoanalyst. He has to sneak under the skin of his characters."[3] It is probably this dark struggle that makes Lang's films different from those of most of his contemporaries, especially in Hollywood. Gavin Lambert suggested that "it is this persistent imaginative projection of an anxiety neurosis that gives Lang's films their unique power."[4]

In a sense the dark struggle becomes a classic encounter between good and evil. The character struggles with a human desire—revenge, illicit love, power—on one hand and the dictates of his conscience on the other. There is pressure to be evil, but there is also pressure to be good. In *Western Union*, for example, Vance Shaw is fleeing from a criminal past and is making an effort to do honest work. He is given a chance by the Western Union Company, and he develops a sense of loyalty to the company boss and to the boss's sister. But when an outlaw band, led, we eventually discover, by

Shaw's brother, begins to prey on the company, Shaw is offered an opportunity to rejoin the gang. He is even suspected by the men of Western Union of working with the thieves. It would have been easy for him to renounce his new life and return to the old one; but his innate sense of decency, perhaps founded on a new-found respect and love, leads him to try to kill his own brother in order to protect the company.

Sometimes the forces of good and evil can be represented in a more subtle manner. In *Metropolis* the real Maria is good; the first time we see her she appears in a slight iris at the door of the Eternal Gardens where the idle rich cavort. The combination of her beatific look, the soft focus of the iris, and her relationship with the children with her gives her the appearance of purity and innocence. Later the false Maria, a robot made to look like the real Maria in order to mislead the workers into violence, appears. She closely resembles her model, but the evil within her alters her appearance, especially when she is performing a sensuous belly dance for a group of ogling sophisticates. The contrast between the real Maria and the false one is a physical manifestation of the confrontation between good and evil. This is the myth of Jekyll and Hyde placed in a futuristic setting: the two Marias represent the two sides of man's nature. The dark struggle between the two sides gives Lang's films their central theme. Perhaps Lang's interest in Expressionism led him to seek exterior symbols for interior struggles.

Fate

Of all the exterior struggles depicted by Lang the one most discussed by the critics and by Lang himself is the one between man and his fate. Even though it is often discussed, it is not always understood; Andrew Sarris realized that an early film *(Metropolis)* and a late one *(Moonfleet)* "share the same bleak view of the universe where man grapples with his personal destiny, and inevitably loses."[5] Sarris has correctly identified fate, or destiny, as a theme that runs the entire length of Lang's career, but he is mistaken in the claim that man "inevitably loses." The Lang character who struggles against his fate is wounded in the struggle, changed by it, but not always defeated by it. For example, the young woman in *Destiny* confronts her fate in the character of Death; but the ending is ambiguous enough to suggest that as she surrenders herself to Death, she is winning through her reunion with her boyfriend.

The problem here is one of definition of the word *fate*. Lang's own attitude explains why the critics have had trouble with this aspect of his work. In an interview he told Nicholas Bartlett how important he thought the struggle against one's fate is: "It seems to me that the general theme of my films is the fight of some individual against what the Greeks and Romans called Fate, which takes the form of some power, a dictatorship, a law, or some crime syndicate."[6] In Greek and Roman theater, Fate remained fate and did not take the form of some human institution, although occasionally some human action might become the agent for Fate. Lang did make use of this type of fate, especially in some of his early films. *Destiny*, for example, contains the story of a woman and her lover who greet Death and try to bargain with him. She is unable to outwit Death, the representation of fate, and finally makes a conscious decision to surrender to it in order to save the life of a child. In the *Nibelungunlied* films Lang makes use of the German legend that Siegfried is fated to die an early death despite his efforts to protect himself from harm. In one of the more memorable scenes in the film, Siegfried bathes in the blood of the slain dragon in order to make his skin impenetrable; as he bathes, a leaf floats down and lands on his back, leaving a small spot untouched by the blood and Siegfried vulnerable. Like Achilles, his life is controlled by fate and no efforts on his part can change that fate.

Siegfried Kracauer sees the attitude toward fate in these two films as the result of the German imagination dwelling on the fear of both tyranny and chaos. According to Kracauer, the Germans believed that the absence of tyranny would lead to chaos and that both states were undesirable: "In this plight contemporaneous imagination resorted to the ancient concept of Fate. Doom decreed by an inexorable Fate was not mere accident but a majestic event that stirred metaphysical shudders in sufferers and witnesses alike."[7]

And this classical fate may be the controlling factor in a number of Lang's early films (Freder seems fated to be the mediator between the brains and the workers in *Metropolis*); but as Lang learned more about psychology and societal influences, he began to create characters who struggle not against the classical Fate, but against some modern representation of it. This is not the Greek or Roman version of fate, but a newer version that is the result of the influences of determinism. In the late nineteenth century writers and scientists put forward the idea that man is controlled by forces outside himself—heredity, the environment, or perhaps fate (Thomas Hardy called this "Hap"). This concept of determinism joined forces with Freudian and Jungian psychology to become a dominant idea in the early part of this century. Fate, as the term applies to Lang's later films, seems to be redefined in light of new insights provided by science and psychology. Fate has come to be represented by specific institutions of man that have come to replace the power of the gods in controlling man's life. Lang wrote: "Fate, with the Greeks and Romans, was their God. Today it is something else; either a dictatorship or a fight against some aspect of society that holds down the individual, or tries to devour him."[8] The struggle of man against some supernatural force, as in *Siegfried*, has become the struggle of man against some aspect of society, as in *The Big Heat*. In both cases the forces are gigantic and man seems small and puny beside them, but the struggle itself is important to Lang.

As Lang makes this shift from one type of fate to another, there is a shift in the type of hero he uses. In his German films the hero is a superman or woman. Lang held that the German military power and the influence of Nietzsche had created a climate in which the central character had to be a superman, such as Siegfried, Dr. Mabuse, or even Freder in *Metropolis*, who is the son of the dictator of the city. But while Lang was working on the screenplay for his first American film, *Fury*, the studio producer talked with him about the central character. Lang had made the man who is attacked by the mob a lawyer, but the producer explained that in America the hero had to be "a man of the people." Lang says he realized that in a country governed by a strong leader or king, the hero has to project the image of the superman who can make no mistakes: "So over there the hero in a motion picture should be a superman, whereas in a democracy he had to be Joe Doe."[9] In his American films the heroes are ordinary people who are caught in a struggle with some new version of fate: for example, Joe in *Fury* is the owner of a service station, Stephen in *Ministry of Fear* is a man just released from a mental hospital, and Christopher Gross in *Scarlet Street* is a bank employee. Thus a shift in the nature of fate is accompanied by a shift in the type of hero; it would be difficult to determine which is the cause and which the effect. It is clear, however, that the two changes had to influence each other and occurred at roughly the same time in Lang's career, along with a change in his political situation.

The substance of the dark struggle, once the focus had shifted away from classical fate and the superman, was the conflict between Joe Doe and the institutions of society that represented this new form of fate. Eddie in *You Only Live Once* is an ex-con who is trying to make an honest living for himself and his new wife. Fate for him is society in general, which has remained suspicious of a man with a criminal past. On their honeymoon Eddie and his wife are asked to leave their carefully chosen cottage when the manager discovers Eddie has been a criminal. Then Eddie is fired by a boss who decides to find a reason to rid his company of an undesirable element. Later Eddie is convicted of robbery and murder largely on the basis of circumstantial evidence and his past record. It is this fate that forces Eddie to return to crime and to kill. It is this fate that leads Eddie and his wife to their deaths in a lonely woods as they try to escape to Mexico and a new beginning.

Fate can be represented by society in general as in *Fury* and *You Only Live Once*, but more often Lang uses a particular group of people or a single person to be the agent of fate. In several films made during World War II, he used the Nazis as the representation of an evil force against which the hero must struggle. In *Man Hunt*, *Hangmen Also Die*, and *The Ministry of Fear*, Lang contrasts men who have succumbed to the enticements of power with other men who continue to struggle against that power no matter what the personal cost.

In some films the group representing fate is smaller. In both *The Return of Frank James* and *Western Union* the heroes encounter small groups of outlaws which become the foes in the struggles. Frank James searches for the Ford brothers to avenge their killing of Jesse; they are the direct and immediate opponents, although society as a whole is held responsible for letting the Fords go free and for creating a situation in which Frank has to do the law's job and punish murderers. In *Western Union* Shaw goes up against a small band of outlaws led by his brother. They are the ones who establish the conflict between the outlaw life and the better life of an employee of Western Union.

Regardless, however, of the nature of the fate or the size of the group representing that fate, the struggle that really counts for Lang is the interior struggle that takes place inside the hero as a result of the external struggle. Fate, no matter what its manifestation, is not the central issue with most of Lang's characters; the struggle with themselves is more important as the exterior opponents are replaced by man's inner self. The exterior struggles are important and interesting, especially in Lang's films that comment on social issues and war, but these struggles achieve thematic significance through the inner struggles they trigger.

Whether the struggle be interior or exterior, the nature of the film medium requires that it be portrayed visually. The interior struggles are the more difficult to depict; that is one reason Lang often resorts to some exterior struggle to represent the interior one, a common trait of expressionism, a style that especially suited his purposes. In *Man Hunt,* for example, the chief struggle seems to be between the Englishman Captain Thorndike and the Nazi officer Quive-Smith, as the latter hunts down the former for an attempt on the life of the Führer. It seems that the struggle is exterior, that is, between the two men and the political stances they represent. But as the film progresses and Quive-Smith forces Thorndike to think about his sporting stalk, the Englishman comes to understand that he did actually intend to kill Hitler and had sublimated the reality. The true struggle is the one within Thorndike as he comes to understand and accept the truth about himself—that he is a man capable of willful and premeditated murder. At this point in the film, he is able to plot and execute the murder of his rival. In this case the exterior struggle between the two men is symbolic of the interior struggle that was Thorndike's alone. Quive-Smith was a suave, calm sadist who had no hesitancy to kill; Thorndike was also suave and calm but thought that he killed only animals. In fact, he tells the German that he had even grown tired of killing animals and preferred the sporting stalk without killing. Thorndike claims that he did not intend to kill Hitler but only to stalk him to see if he really were the hunter he was supposed to be. It takes Thorndike some time to realize that Quive-Smith represents that inner side of himself that is actually willing to kill a man.

Plot Devices to Present "the Dark Struggle"

There are certain plot devices which Lang resorts to on numerous occasions that present the struggles, both interior and exterior. These become characteristic of his plots in enough films to become familiar ingredients in the struggles. In other words, Lang, when he wants to depict a character in a struggle, often resorts to several favorite plot situations: violence, hallucinations, mistaken identity, and religion.

A. Violence

A most obvious and widely discussed device is Lang's use of violence. The exterior struggle, since it most often places people in conflict, naturally leads to fights and other acts of violence. Some of the most memorable scenes in *Kriemhild's Revenge* are those of the battle between the troops of Kriemhild and Attila and the forces of her brothers. We remember vividly the banquet hall as she burns it down over the heads of her fallen family and former friends.

Murder in many forms, armed robbery, accidental death, arson, and beatings characterize the violence between men and women in Lang's films that is part of the exterior struggles, but none is so memorable or symbolic as that in *The Big Heat*. Vince Stone, the muscle man for hoodlum Mike Lagana, indulges his sadistic tastes in a number of ways; but the horror of the scene in which he throws boiling coffee in the face of his beautiful girl friend elicits a personal response from the viewers that is not even matched by the burning of the banquet hall in *Kriemhild's Revenge*. We feel the pain as Debbie runs from him screaming, unable to assuage the pain. The evil in this man has destroyed beauty and created an atmosphere of horror that is not diminished until she revenges herself by throwing coffee in his face late in the film.

As frightening as the physical violence is, psychological violence is more interesting to a director who likes to expose his characters to stress and observe their reactions; thus psychological violence becomes the most threatening form in Lang's films. The criminals in *M* reduce the murderer to a psychologically babbling mess until he realizes that his only hope is to face them with their own smugness. In *Metropolis* the true Maria is chased in the basement of Rotwang's house in a scene in which the only light is a flashlight that picks her out of the darkness. In *The Last Will of Dr. Mabuse* the mad doctor does violence to the mind of Dr. Baum by hypnotizing him into acting as his agent in crime. And in *The Ministry of Fear* the Nazis attempt to convince Stephen, who has just been released from an asylum, that he is in fact still insane.

Generally this violence is directed against other people, but occasionally it is directed against objects. In *Western Union* some of the violence is against the company itself and its wagon train, which is finally burned out by outlaws. In *Metropolis* the violence is directed against the machines, which have come to represent the authority of the ruling class to the workmen.

Most of this violence represents the exterior struggles, but Lang is capable of using violence to represent the interior struggle as well. In *You Only Live Once*, Eddie stands in his cell just hours before his scheduled execution and slowly cuts his wrist with a piece of tin. This beautifully structured scene does demonstrate Eddie's defiance of the outer world as represented by the prison, but it also shows the struggle within himself as he hurts himself in order to win his struggle with the outer world. In *Western Union* Shaw performs much the same act as he burns ropes off his wrist in order to escape from his capture by the outlaw gang. He too seems to be punishing himself for his bad side that allowed him to be captured and that left the wagon train vulnerable.

Lang has a reputation as a director who makes excessive use of violence, but such criticism fails to take into account his own understanding of the art of the cinema. Lang's films do seem violent, but not in the vein of the blood and gore that so characterizes the films of latter-day filmmakers, such as Sam Peckinpah. Lang made the violence a part of the theme of the dark struggle. He told an interviewer that he does not use violence for its own sake: "In these days when people no longer have religious beliefs, when we no longer believe in Hell, the only thing we fear is pain, and pain is the result of violence in some form or other."[10] Fear, pain, and violence—the three are united as the central device for depicting the struggles. In the tradition of the classical Greek theater, the violence is rarely seen. In *M* a ball that rolls out of a bush indicates that the murderer has another young victim. In *You Only Live Once* the camera is on Eddie's face as he cuts his wrist. We see the pain, not the act of violence. In *Man Hunt* we see the shadows as the Nazis beat and torture Thorndike and we see his beaten body, but we do not directly see the violence. Even in *The Big Heat*, we do not actually see the coffee hit Debbie's face; and the explosion that kills Bannion's wife and sends him on his rampage for revenge is only a flash at the window as he reads a bedtime story to their daughter. The violence is more suggested than shown. Lang knew that it could be more effective on the viewer done that way; he leaves it to us to imagine the horror of the violence. Through our imaginations we become his collaborators in the creation of horror.

Lang's violent movies are tempered with tenderness, as Nicholas Bartlett further points out.[11] *Fury* opens with the young couple looking at bedroom furniture and ends with their kiss. Professor Novotny, in *Hangmen Also Die!*, calmly bids his family and students good-bye as he is being taken off to a Nazi prison. These scenes, and others, tend to keep the films from being so resolutely violent, but at the same time they also heighten the violence through contrast. The contrast between the tough cop reading a bedtime story to his daughter and the explosion outside the window makes the murder of Bannion's wife more horrible.

B. Hallucination

One of the devices of plot Lang uses to depict the special power of the dark struggle is hallucination. Frequently a Lang character who is under special stress, especially a stress caused by an interior struggle, will have some type of psychological visions that will give the character himself, or perhaps the viewers, insights into the character. This hallucination then becomes a visual representation of what is going on in the mind or the subconscious of the character, a cinematic equivalent of the use of the soliloquy in Elizabethan theater.

Often this hallucination takes the form of a dream which shows viewers the psychological fears and fantasies of the dreamer. For instance, almost the entirety of *Woman in the Window* turns out to be a dream. We are shown a lonely professor reading at his club after having dinner and a few drinks with some male friends. He leaves the club, meets a woman on the street, becomes involved with her, commits murder because of her, and covers up his crime. Just as he is about to be caught, he wakes up and we discover that he had actually fallen asleep in the club and had dreamed this crime and his pursuit by the police. While there is some argument over the cinematic effectiveness of such a surprise ending, it is true that the dreams of a slightly drunk and lonely middle-aged man suggest fantasies not unknown to many men.

The dream hallucination is used differently in *Siegfried*. Early in the film, before Kriemhild has even met Siegfried, she has a dream that portends the tragedy in the future of her lover-to-be. In this dream a white dove fills the screen and then is attacked by two black hawks. The white dove is symbolic of Siegfried, who has been dressed in white and who has blond hair. He is to be attacked by Hagan and Brunhild, who are dressed in dark colors, like the hawks, and who wear helmets with wings for embellishment.

Sometimes the hallucination is dreamlike but inspired by illness rather than sleep. In *Metropolis* Feder has suffered a long illness as a result of his conflict with Rotwang. He stirs in his bed but seems to remain in a semiconscious state for some time. During this period he has visions of the false Maria as she entertains the company at Rotwang's party with her sensuous belly dance while standing on a platform supported by half-naked black slaves. Later during the vision, the slaves turn into the figures of the seven deadly sins that have been seen earlier in the cathedral. The vision changes into a dance of death as the figure of death leads the seven deadly sins in an eerie performance. Exhausted from his vision, Feder falls back onto his pillow and sleeps.

Sometimes the hallucinations in Lang's films are inspired by guilt. A character undergoing psychological stress caused by guilt for actions he has performed may hallucinate and have visions that reflect

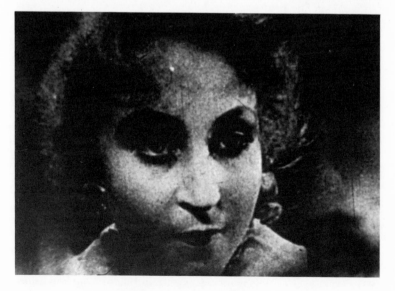

Metropolis: The false Maria as a darkened seductress

the guilt. These are the strangest of the hallucinations used by Lang;
those inspired by dreams or illness are easily accepted by the audience because many people have experienced strange visions while
asleep or ill. But the hallucinations which reveal guilt are different.
They may occur to a Lang character while he is walking down the
street or driving his car. For instance, at the end of *Fury*, Joe has left
the hotel room after an argument with his brothers and Katherine.
He tries to lose himself in a cheap bar. When the bartender accidentally rips too many sheets off the wall calendar and reveals the wrong
date, the number twenty-two comes up, the number of defendants
Joe is sending to their deaths with his plan for convicting them of his
murder. The number brings the guilt from the subconscious to the
conscious, and he runs out of the bar into the street. There he
pauses in front of a window of a flower store and begins to hallucinate. The screenplay describes what happens: "Ghostly forms seem
to materialize at Joe's back, looking over his shoulder. They have
the faces of Dawson, the woman and others of the defendants. He
stands motionless, hearing whispering voices."[12] The experience
destroys the outward calm and assurance Joe has maintained up to
this point, and he runs back to the gloomy flat seeking security and
forgiveness. The next morning he confesses.

Guilt also causes the major hallucination in *The Last Will of Dr.
Mabuse*. Dr. Baum has become the agent for Dr. Mabuse's crimes,
but the police have spotted him and have begun to chase him. As
Dr. Baum drives away, the viewers get the first glimpse of the
hallucination. The car seems to move with reckless speed, the trees
at the roadside take on a strange appearance, and the set becomes
an unnatural white color. Suddenly over Baum's shoulder appears
Dr. Mabuse whispering, "Failed, failed." Baum goes to his hospital
office where he again encounters Dr. Mabuse, who hands him a
sheet of paper and tells him, "You failed." Slowly the faces of the
two men merge into one as Baum goes completely insane.

The use of hallucination is especially appropriate for a director
who works with man's inner struggles. The hallucination depicts
well what is happening in a man's mind and reflects the stress
caused by the struggle.

C. Mistaken Identity

Since the struggles of Lang's films are characterized by Jekyll-
Hyde exchanges of personality, it is natural that on some occasions

there will be confusion of character. In a psychological drama when one side of the person's character is exchanged for another, there may not be an accompanying physical change to symbolize the inner change, as there was in the original Jekyll-Hyde myth. In other words, the character may change, but another person looking at the changed person may not be able to discern the change simply from the character's physical appearance. In *The Last Will of Dr. Mabuse* just described it becomes apparent that the evilness of Dr. Mabuse takes over the person of Dr. Baum and dominates his character making him perform evil acts. It is impossible until the end to tell that Dr. Baum is any different. This same device is repeated in *The Thousand Eyes of Dr. Mabuse*, the last of the Mabuse films, in which the kindly Dr. Jordan turns out to be the genius behind a criminal plan to take over the world. Dr. Jordan has been inspired by Mabuse.

Much the same type of mistaken identity is used in *Ministry of Fear*, in which Willi Hilfe pretends to befriend Stephen. Eventually Stephen learns that his friend is a Nazi spy who is using him and is trying to kill him. In many of the war films, in fact, the mistaken-identity device is used by people on the side of the allies to fool and confuse the enemy. In *Man Hunt* Thorndike tells his brother, who is an official in the British government, that he will assume a new identity in order not to embarrass the government as the man who tried to assassinate Hitler. In *Hangmen Also Die!* Dr. Svobada hides his true identity and gives a false name to Mascha and her family in order to protect both them and himself. Then in *Cloak and Dagger* Professor Jasper becomes a secret agent for the American government and takes a new identity in order to go under cover into Nazi territory. In these cases the mistaken identity is not the result of evilness, but in all cases it is either the cause of some interior struggle (as in Svobada's conflict over whether he should save innocent people and reveal himself) or the result of the external struggle (as with Thorndike).

In these cases perhaps hidden identity is a more accurate term than mistaken identity because each of the people is careful to see that other characters mistake their identity. War settings are not, however, the only ones in which Lang uses this device of plot. In *Rancho Notorious* Vern Haskell goes into a criminals' lair in order to find the murderer of his girl and naturally does not reveal his true identity.

The mistaken, or hidden, identity is, of course, a means of expressing the two sides of a person's character, and literature is full of such plot devices. When, however, a director repeatedly uses the device to symbolize the two good and evil sides of his characters, the device takes on a special significance in his work.

D. Christian Symbols

Lang seems to have become convinced that religion was no longer important enough to most people to make it the basis for a central struggle in his films, but he did on occasion use Christian symbols to reinforce his theme and to make a statement about the struggle. It seems that he used religion as a metaphor to explain the depth of the struggle.

Metropolis is heavily religious, for example. Lang makes use of the biblical myths of the Tower of Babel, the Garden of Eden, and the Flood to represent the evilness of the cities and to set up the New Testament goodness of Maria and Feder. The symbolism of Maria's name matches the description of her in the shot analysis: "Maria stares straight at the camera, goodness and tenderness shining from her Madonnalike eyes; then she spreads her arms wide, looking up to heaven, and begins to speak."[13] This description is taken from the scene in which we first see Maria standing in the catacombs beneath the city. She is seen in front of an altar covered with candles. During her sermon she tells the workers that a mediator must come to find the compromise between the workers and management. It is as though she has come as John the Baptist to prepare the way for Feder, who will become the mediator. By the end of the film Feder has saved Maria, protected the children, and gotten labor and management to shake hands. In the final scene he is dressed all in white and stands between his father, the management, and Grot, the representative of the workers, both of whom are dressed in dark clothes. Had it not been for the teachings and support of Maria, Feder would not have been in this position; in a sense she gave birth to him. Feder as a Christ metaphor serves to reinforce the need of the heart to unite the brains and strength. The struggle between the two opposing forces must be reconciled by the Christlike actions of the heart. As Maria says in her sermon: "Between the brain that plans and the hands that build, there must be a mediator . . . . It is the heart that must bring an understanding between them."[14]

But the use of a religious metaphor was not restricted to Lang's early films. In *You Only Live Once* he uses a religious idea to tone down the brutality of the ending. One of Eddie's chief supporters at the prison was the priest who volunteers to try to talk Eddie out of trying to escape. The priest comes to Eddie out of the darkness in a heavy mist or fog and has his arms spread in a Christlike configuration. He begs Eddie to reconsider and to believe he is a free man, proven innocent of murder. Eddie does not believe and accidentally kills the priest and escapes. In the final scene, Eddie is carrying his dead wife into the woods near the Mexican border when he is shot. As he staggers, dying, the woods take on a special glow as light penetrates their darkness. The voice of the priest is heard in Eddie's mind saying, "You're free, Eddie. The gates are open." In this case, the priest has been the Christ figure and has offered Eddie the peace he never found in this life.

In *Hangmen Also Die!* the most ridiculed and despised character in the film surprisingly takes on additional significance at the end of the film through a Christ metaphor. Czaka, the very unChristlike collaborator with the Nazis, is framed for the murder of Heydrich, the Reichsprotektor, by the Czech patriots whom he has betrayed. The Nazis accept the frame because there is little chance to find the real killer. They take Czaka for a ride, stop the car, and tell him to run; when he does, they naturally shoot him. He runs a few steps further and comes to the steps of a church. He mounts a few of the steps and dies there, with his arms outspread as though he were on the cross. Organ music reinforces the visuals. There is little preparation for this Christ metaphor in the film and its inclusion probably is unimportant to most viewers, if, in fact, they see it at all. Lang, however, probably used the image here in order to make the point that Czaka is a scapegoat dying for the sins of all the Nazis. His sins were universal, and his death symbolizes his relation with Nazis yet to die.

Even though Lang did not see religion as a continuing powerful force in modern life, he found in it symbols that could be universally understood.

Mythology as Reinforcement of "the Dark Struggle"

Lang was a director who was keenly aware of the literary, social, and cultural traditions that have created the milieus in which he made his films. Since his films reflected the traditions which influenced him, it was natural that he should make use of archetypes as one means of expressing and reinforcing the dark struggles. Many filmmakers obviously reflect their mythology subconsciously, but Lang used myths and archetypes consciously.

His films are dotted by easily recognized archetypes, characters and experiences that are representatives of the perceptions we hold in common and express through our dreams and art forms. These archetypes in Lang's films become central to the conflicts that make up the struggles. A few examples will serve to illustrate the point. Lang frequently calls upon the archetype of the superman, a character that is often responsible for the conflict in his films. Supermen, such as Dr. Mabuse or Haighi in *Spies*, are actually the source of conflict in their films, the characters who force others to confront evil and to experience the struggle. As the source of conflict, the superman is actively involved in it and represents one side of the struggle. On the other hand, the seductress, another of Lang's archetypes, is frequently the cause of the conflict and struggle in his films, but usually not as directly involved as a participant as is the superman. In *Woman in the Window* and *Scarlet Street* Lang's male characters are drawn into an affair with seductresses, but the affair is only part of the struggle for these men and not nearly as important to them as the crimes they commit as a result of the affairs. The struggle belongs to the men, not to the women who were partly to blame for it. Similarly in Lang's films the virgin is usually not directly involved in the struggle, but she is supportive of her man whose struggle concerns her. In *Fury* Katherine is a well-developed character, but the struggle belongs to her boyfriend, Joe. Similar women offer their love and support to the heroes in their struggles in *Western Union*, *The Return of Frank James*, and *Ministry of Fear*. Another archetype that is important in Lang's social-comment films is the scapegoat, the character that takes on the guilt of society. Joe in *Fury* is typical (as is Eddie in *You Only Live Once* and Czaka in *Hangmen Also Die!*). After the citizens of Sage County have set the jail on fire, they gather to watch the blaze. Joe appears at one of the windows and the people pick up stones and throw them at him, the rocks bouncing off the wall and bars near his head. There is no particular reason for them to throw rocks as he cannot escape through the window, but symbolically their action identifies them with others through the centuries who have found a nameless person to become the scapegoat providing relief for their own guilt. At the end of the trial, as the woman breaks down and confesses, she screams hysterically: "I can't stand it anymore, I can't stand it! I want to confess—I threw stones at him, I helped kill him!"

Lang also involves his characters in retellings of well-known myths that tend to heighten the struggles and make them more universal. He uses the myths of the Tower of Babel and the Garden of Eden in *Metropolis* and the story of the Nibelungen treasure in the Nibelungen Saga. Some myths he uses without naming, such as the Flood and Holocaust in *Metropolis* and Beauty and the Beast in *The Big Heat*. These myths are statements of conflict, and their narratives describe the struggles that are familiar to most men, at least in their subconscious form. The ancient myth of Beauty and the Beast, for example, describes the struggle of a beautiful young woman to accept the love of an extremely ugly beast. Once she learns that his love and concern are of more value to her than the good looks she hoped for, the two are able to give to each other and exchange love. This myth is central to *The Big Heat* and helps to explain the struggle that is going on in the mind of Dave Bannion. As a policeman he is trying to solve several related crimes, not the least of which is the murder of his wife. Debbie, the girl friend of one of the gangsters suspected of the crimes, offers friendship, which Bannion rejects, despite her beauty, because of her connections with Vince Stone. Later, when Stone throws the coffee in her face, Debbie becomes a visual manifestation of the Beauty and the Beast. One side of her face is scarred and ugly; the other is still beautiful. This time when she goes to Bannion, he understands what she is offering and is able to accept her friendship, perhaps even her love. The two together are able to solve the crimes and punish the guilty. Debbie remains the personification of the myth to the end as the Beauty side of her loves Bannion; the Beast side is capable of violence which ultimately resolves the situation.

The myth of Jekyll and Hyde which Lang had wanted to turn into *The Man Behind You* becomes then a metaphor for all the struggles Lang chose as his chief cinematic material. Lang's characters struggle with the exterior forces that try to control them, but finally the struggle within and the victory over the forces that cause that struggle are the central substance of his films.

3

The Camera and the Struggle

AN UNDERSTANDING of Lang's central theme of struggle depends in part on the appreciation of the plots and myths created by Lang and his screenwriters, but also important to this understanding is an awareness of Lang's expertise as a film director.

The film is, naturally enough, the sum total of the parts that go into it. The experience of viewing a film is complex; the viewer absorbs the narrative by hearing the actors speak their lines and by watching them move on the screen, but these experiences do not constitute the total film experience. The viewer is also influenced and manipulated by the technical skill of the director and the crew he has assembled. The viewer may be conscious of the fact that the actors tell and show him the story, but he may not be conscious of the fact that the use of color, sound, editing, and the rest of the director's bag of tricks contributes to the understanding of the story and to the appreciation of the work of art.

Fritz Lang was consciously using the art of the medium to do more than just tell a story; he found ways to use the techniques to reinforce the theme of "the dark struggle" that was central to his work. He was able to create a feeling for the struggle that did not come from what a character said or did, but rather from what was shown on the screen. This ability is at the heart of what it is to be a film and is that which distinguishes a film from a novel or a drama. In other words, Lang was a master at the craft of making pictures.

For the convenience of this discussion, the techniques that help to depict the dark struggle can be divided into two categories: the first consists of those associated with the camera; the second consists of techniques needed to create a set and other objects for the camera to photograph.

M: *The shadow of the murderer falls across the poster advertising the missing girl*

Technique

A. Lighting

Most of Lang's movies were shot in black and white, but Lang was a master at playing off the contrasts created by the light and the dark, at finding just the right light to illuminate partly dark figures moving through an even heavier darkness, or at allowing background light to be just strong enough to permit the viewer to discern what is going on in the foreground. Lang's use of light and dark to create a mood or to emphasize a point of character leaves a strong impression on the eye and mind of the viewer. Generally Lang created a contrast between good and evil through the use of light; more often than not, Lang's heroes are bathed in white, or at least shades of light gray, while the villains are dressed in dark clothes with little light added artistically. One very fine example is the scene of Siegfried's murder in the first part of the Nibelungen Saga. Earlier Hagan has plotted to kill Siegfried and has tricked Kriemhild into marking the vunerable spot on Siegfried's back with a cross sewn onto Siegfried's tunic. Then after the hunt, when Siegfried complains of thirst that only water will quench, Hagan challenges Siegfried to a footrace to the spring and carefully allows Siegfried to race ahead. Siegfried arrives at the spring and falls down to drink. Lang has him dressed in white and has fully lighted the pool and waterfall that are in the background. The pool is surrounded by white birch trees, and the combination gives a scene that is full of whiteness and warmth. Suddenly, the camera cuts to Hagan, who has come up behind Siegfried. Hagan is dressed in black and is standing behind a dark tree. In order to emphasize the darkness of this man, Lang has silhouetted him against a light sky that appears in the upper right of the frame. The contrast between the goodness of Siegfried and the evilness of Hagan is depicted here visually, and the viewer senses at once that the time has come for the final physical struggle between these two men. The fight does not last long as Hagan throws his dark spear into Siegfried's white back.

The contrast between good and evil is depicted in *You Only Live Once* in a slightly different way. In this case good and evil are represented by contrasting one man against blackness. The night Eddie attempts to escape from the prison is full of fog. Even when there are lights to break through the heavy blackness, there are still patches of fog to obscure the light and make it hazy. Out of the blackness and fog comes Father Dolan. Lang has him backlighted so that the combination of fog, light, and darkness creates a glow around the priest. This glow and the attitude of his arms creates the Christlike appearance discussed in Chapter 2.

The result of the contrast of light and darkness is, of course, shadows; and at times Lang uses shadows specifically to denote evil. In *Man Hunt* the Nazi Quive-Smith has ordered his henchmen to beat and torture Captain Thorndike, who has refused to sign a document implicating his government in his assassination attempt. The viewers do not see the torture, but instead the shadow of a man who is being beaten. The implication here is that the evil is too horrible to show.

But it is in *M* that Lang had his most memorable use of a shadow. Lang spends much time in this film establishing an atmosphere of fear. We, as viewers, come to understand that some perverted man is preying on the young girls in the city. A young girl leaves school and dawdles on her way home, playing with her ball. She begins bouncing her ball off of a white poster that offers a reward for the killer and warns mothers to be careful about not neglecting their children. The girl and the poster are bathed in light. Suddenly, without warning, the shadow of a man crosses the poster and the girl turns to stare at the man. The appearance of the shadow both startles and saddens us as we sense at once that the shadow belongs to the killer.

Sometimes Lang was able to use a flashing light to represent the struggle between good and evil. In *Scarlet Street* the bank employee Christopher Cross has allowed another man to die in the electric chair for a murder Cross committed. Right after the man has been taken, protesting his innocence, through the steel doors leading to the execution room, the next shot is of a cheap hotel room. The room is dark except for the light provided by a blinking neon sign outside the room, advertising the hotel. The light reveals Cross, who goes crazy as the light blinks on him. He hallucinates as he sees in his mind's eye his girl friend and her lover in an assignation. We hear their voices from the next world and Cross talks with them. He tells Kitty that she is pure but that her boyfriend is evil. Through all of this the light has continued to flash, creating an unreal appearance to the room and emphasizing the growing insanity of Cross. This scene is important to Lang because it shows the full extent of the punishment of a man who has committed several crimes and yet not been convicted and punished by the law. The Hays office, of course, required that all guilty people be punished, but Lang says that he had no trouble with this film because Cross suffers so greatly.[1] The flashing light becomes a visual representation of the confusion in Cross's mind that causes the suffering. A similar flashing light is used to create a portentous mood in *The Blue Gardenia*, in which the meeting between Norah and Casey, the reporter, takes place in a darkened newspaper city room, lighted only by the flashing neon name of the paper.

Finally, Lang uses light to highlight a character and to emphasize the struggle that is taking place between that person and the darkness that surrounds him or her. The most memorable example is that of Maria in *Metropolis*. She is the last one to leave the catacombs after her speech to the workers and is trapped in the cavern by Rotwang. Her candle is snuffed out, and she is lighted only by the beam from his torch. This round beam, more like the beam from a flashlight than from a torch, finds her in the dark and follows her as she runs, looking frantically for the door. Out of the darkness comes that beam, illuminating the fright on her face and freezing her like a deer that has been startled in the night by the headlights of a car.

Like nineteenth-century novelists, such as Hawthorne, Lang has used the contrast between light and darkness to emphasize the contrast between good and evil. He has used black and white characteristics inherent in his medium to heighten the struggles that are central to his films and has, in other words, taken advantage of the medium and made it fit his thematic purposes as well as his narrative needs.

B. Color

Black and white films seem best suited to express the subtleties of the theme of the dark struggle, but Lang was not unaware of the potential for color. He made six color films: *The Return of Frank James, Western Union, An American Guerrilla in the Philippines, Rancho Notorious, Moonfleet,* and *The Hindu Tomb*. At times his use of color was remarkable.

Lang's color films use color to highlight and symbolize, much the same technique as when he used shadows and lights in the black and white films. The fire that destroys the wagons in *Western Union* is both beautiful and fearful as the yellow and orange flames break out of the black night. And in *Rancho Notorious* the blackness of Altar Keane's dress is deepened through contrast with the color of the world that surrounds her.

At times Lang's use of color could be too subtle. He says that in *Western Union* he used shades of yellow and violet because those were the colors of telegrams.[2]

C. Sound

Of the thirty-nine films Lang directed, twelve (counting the films with two parts as single films) were silent. Good directors such as Lang were able to create an aura of sound even when the actors spoke no words and the audience's imaginations had to provide the special-effect sounds of guns going off and giant cities exploding. Kevin Brownlow has reminded us in *The Parade's Gone By* that the silent movies were never really silent. And, of course, there was a musical score provided for a piano or orchestral accompaniment for the movie. The opening of *Siegfried* in New York was enlivened by a sixty-piece orchestra that played a score improvised from Wagner;[3] surely the music of Wagner and the visuals of Lang created a spectacle that can never be recaptured (it cannot be the same as the live performance in New York, but Blackhawk Films now releases a print of *Siegfried* with a Wagnerian soundtrack).

Whatever the aesthetics of the silent films may be, the silent-film director was obviously limited in his use of sound; and when sound was introduced, Lang found a new technique that he could use to enhance his art and to present better his central theme. Even in his first sound film, *M*, Lang was able to demonstrate a skill in the cinematic use of sound that ably complements his stylized visuals. Critic Lotte Eisner, in an article that shows deep understanding of Lang's style, lists the sound images in *M* that stick out in her mind, sort of an aural image scan: "the song so dismally dreary in the mouths of playing children, floating in their shrill voices across the courtyards of the slums; the mother's call for the missing child ebbing away in the sickening hollowness of the staircase; some jerky measures of Grieg's troll-melody whistled again and again as a sinister leitmotiv whenever the pervert appears. . . ."[4]

Lang quickly learned methods of using this new technique to help him represent the struggle. In *Fury*, for example, the contrast between silence and noise helps to identify the goodness of Katherine as opposed to the evilness of the mob. In the scene in which the mob burns the jail, there is a great deal of noise. There is a fight between the sheriff's men and the mob which is accompanied by shouts and the breaking of doors and furniture. The sacking of the jail and the fire itself also contribute to the sounds. Then once the camera has followed the mob outside, two men throw sticks of dynamite into the blaze, causing an explosion. All of this sound is contrasted with the silence of Katherine as she runs toward the jail. In the shots of her, all we hear is the sound of her running and her feeble cries to passing cars for help. Compared to the scenes of the mob, the noise here is foreboding in its absence. There is a clear visual contrast between the mob, which is acting as a more or less anonymous unit, and the lone girl struggling to arrive at the jail before her boyfriend is harmed, but these visuals are reinforced by the soundtrack.

This use of silence to contrast with sound is effectively used in other films as well. As mentioned in Chapter 2, *You Only Live Once* and *Western Union* contain scenes in which the heroes injure their wrists in order to free themselves, one from jail and the other from the ropes that bind him. Both of these scenes are painful ones in which the audience suffers with the men and feels their hurt. Quite appropriately, there is little sound at these moments—the tearing of the cup to use as a weapon or the crackling of the fire, sounds that contribute to the horror of what the audience is seeing. But the most memorable use of silence in the sound films comes in *An American Guerrilla in the Philippines*. One of the American soldiers is hiding from the Japanese soldiers and scrunches under a log. As the enemy soldiers poke around in the underbrush with their bayonets, the camera is on the lone soldier. The only sounds are those of the Japanese men as the American tries very hard to keep still. Suddenly we realize that ants have begun to attack the man under the log and that they have swarmed over his leg. The look on his face and the anguish in his eyes tell us how badly he wants to move, to run, to scream; his silence is eloquent. The absence of sound when ordinarily there would be sound depicts the seriousness of the struggle the soldier undergoes.

Naturally the soundtrack is used to convey the voices of Lang's characters discussing their struggles, but at times he uses the voices imaginatively. For instance he likes to use the voiceover, in which a voice comes over the soundtrack to provide either a narrative link or a view into the mind of the character, sort of a twentieth-century soliloquy. In *An American Guerilla in the Philippines* the voiceover is of a narrator who connects the film's various episodes by filling in the narrative not shown. Despite the fact that this narrator describes the struggles between the opposing forces of the war, this narration seems dull and overly pompous. The voiceover in *Scarlet Street* is much more effective. As indicated above, having successfully gotten Kitty's boyfriend to be executed for her murder, Cross goes insane in his hotel room. His mental state is caused by his guilt and frustration; the flashing lights represent visually this insanity. But at the same time Cross hears voices and carries on a conversation with the long-dead Kitty.

D. Shots

One of the basic decisions a director has to make concerns the selection of the shots to be photographed by the camera. There are, of course, many considerations to be made before deciding on the particular shot to be used, many of which have little to do with theme; but Lang often selected shots that would specifically reinforce or establish the struggles that were taking place. Examples from three films will give a brief idea of his methods.

In *Western Union*, a film not generally notable for its memorable camera shots, there are two pan shots that call attention to the conflict that is developing on camera. The first concerns three white men who have come to make peace with hostile Indians who have forbidden Western Union to take telegraph poles through Indian territory. The camera is sitting on the wagon trail, focused on the approaching wagon with the three men. Then it tilts upward to the telegraph wire, reminding us that this wire is the center of the argument between the two groups. It follows the wire until it comes to a pole. Then it tilts down the pole, showing that the wire has come to an end and is curled up on the ground beside the last pole. The shot continues down the wagon trail in the opposite direction and reveals Indians in full war dress waiting on the trail. This is a 180° pan. The camera began by showing the wagon coming from one direction and ended up, in a single shot, by showing the Indians in exactly the opposite direction. The opposing sides of this struggle have been brought together in a single shot and set up as opposites through their geographical placement.

Later in the same film Lang uses a similar shot to establish the scene in which Shaw has to fight his brother and three other outlaws. The camera is inside a barber shop, revealing the four men. Without moving, it shows through the window Shaw outside on the street walking toward the shop. Because this is a long shot and because he is framed by the large window, he appears to be very small and lonely—one man against four. The camera follows Shaw as he walks toward the shop and then pans to show him walking through the door and into the shop. This has been a pan of perhaps 100 or 110°, not as long as the one described above, but more effective because it first establishes Shaw's isolation and the odds against him before it brings him into direct confrontation with the men, the major struggle in the film.

In *M* Lang uses an interesting contrast between the effectiveness of the long shot and the effectiveness of the close-up. Once the murderer has been identified, he begins to run. There is a famous shot of him during the chase, which is a long shot taken from high up on one of the buildings. We see the murderer run into an empty street. From this distance he is very small and almost unidentifiable. Like Shaw, he is isolated by the shot. He then runs this way and then that, finding his way blocked no matter which way he goes. This shot reveals his loss of identity and his frustrations.

Later at the trial Lang uses the close-up not just to give the murderer back his identity, but to portray at the same time the man's continuing frustrations. The looks on his face as seen in extreme close-up show us his fear, his self-degradation, and finally a hint of defiance as he tells his captors they have no right to judge him as they do not understand the compulsions that drive him.

The close-up was used effectively in *Fury* to give a certain individuality to the people who make up the mob. In the mob scenes in *Metropolis* all the people are completely anonymous, but in *Fury* the mob is even more horrible because the people in it are given personality. This is a mob all right, but it is made up of individuals who later will have to pay for their participation. Lang gives us close-ups of the woman holding her child, of the man eating a hot-dog, of an old woman praying. These shots add a dimension to the struggle between Joe and the mob. When he seeks his revenge for the injustices done to him, he is not asking for the deaths of anonymous nobodies, but of real people who laugh and eat and pray. The evilness of Joe's actions is therefore heightened, regardless of the evil these people have done to him.

E. Editing

Once the camera work has been done, the next stage for the director is to edit the film and put his shots in the proper sequence.

Early practitioners of the film arts realized that there is some special relationship that exists among shots—the montage effect—that suggests that the total effect on the viewer is the result not only of the viewing of the individual shots but also of the viewer's perception of the interrelationships of the shots. Lang and his editors have made special use of editing in order to emphasize the various conflicts basic to the plots. In *M*, for example, once the crime has been committed, both the police and the ordinary crooks of the city determine to capture the murderer. Each group develops its own plan for finding him and a race is on to see which group is successful. One of the struggles of the film then is between these two groups. In order to depict the struggle, Lang uses the editing technique of crosscutting between the two groups. He will show a scene or two of the crooks and their search, then a few scenes of the police and their efforts to restore law and order. Then back to the crooks, back to the police, and so on. This method establishes a direct counterbalance between the two groups; it is the cinematic equivalent of the musical counterpoint. The effect is heightened by Lang's having both groups performing the same acts. What one group does is paralleled in the next sequence by a similar action performed by the other group. For instance, the sequence in which the crooks' leaders plan their actions against the murderer is followed by a sequence in which the police leaders make their plans.

A rather obvious metaphor is created in *Fury* through the use of editing. After Joe has been arrested, the rumors of his guilt spread rapidly through the town through the typical small-town grapevine. Lang shows us the women as they run quickly to their phones to be the first to tell what they know and even a bit of what they do not know. Then he shows us the marketplace, where the gossip gathers momentum in the presence of a high concentration of eager receivers and conveyers of news. In one shot he shows a group of the women as they maliciously chatter away. Then he cuts to a shot of a group of geese as they honk about the barnyard. This seemingly strange technique is an old one borrowed from the Russians, but the metaphoric meaning is clear, if a bit trite by today's standards. Lang later admitted that American audiences did not need this obvious instruction, as did some European ones.[5]

More effective in stating the struggle is the sort of editing through contrast that Lang uses in *You Only Live Once*. The girl, Jo, has gone to the prison to try to see her husband, who believes that she betrayed him when she talked him into giving himself up to the police. The camera is on her as she goes up to the steel door with a small square hole in it for communication with the prisoners. In this shot she is full size as she nervously waits for Eddie to come. Suddenly Lang cuts to the other side of the door and gives us a shot from Eddie's point of view. Seen from this side, only Jo's head is visible in the middle of a geometrically balanced door. She appears small and isolated, surrounded by steel. Eddie is the one in prison, but this shot makes it appear that Jo is also locked up. She has, metaphorically, become the prisoner of her love for a doomed man. The struggle between these two people and, additionally, the struggle within Jo is highlighted by the relationship of these two shots, one from each side of the steel door.

In a long career of a director with Lang's talent, there are countless examples of editing that could be cited as examples of his artistry. These few samples only serve to illustrate his ability to combine his instincts for good camera shots with his thematic needs.

F. Experiments

"Experiments" is something of a misnomer for this section, but there seems to be no better term to describe Lang's attempts to combine several of the technical devices discussed above in order to achieve unusual effects. Shots, editing, and light can be brought together in different ways to achieve effects not ordinarily seen in narrative feature films. Lang did not, however, invent these effects and they are therefore not strictly experimental. Lang did know how to borrow effects from experimental filmmakers and to use those effects to highlight his struggles.

In *Destiny,* for example, he added to the supernatural character of the Death figure by having him disappear through a solid wall, a simple trick developed by George Méliès in the first decade of this century. In *Siegfried* the sequence in which the two black hawks attack the white dove is animated, a nice effect achieved through contrast with the live-action sequences that surround it. These "experimental" effects are especially valuable to Lang when he is trying to create the effect of hallucination discussed in Chapter 2. Dream sequences and flashbacks in a number of films were created through changing the speed of the camera, altering the amount of light available, or devising a collage of unusual images (such as the eyes that open *The Thousand Eyes of Dr. Mabuse*).

What the Camera Sees

What is done with the camera, lighting, and film is only one part of the technical considerations that go into the making of a film; the other part is concerned with what it is that the camera photographs. Lang's films are highly regarded for his ability to create distinctive visuals that highlight his actors. From the point of view of this study the important visuals are the ones that significantly reinforce the struggles among and within the characters on the screen.

A. Architecture

As mentioned in Chapter 1, Lang's father was an architect and Lang himself had for a time been destined for this profession before filmmaking enticed him away. He never lost his feel for buildings. His love of design and those early interests of his carried over into filmmaking and gave his films one of their most distinctive characteristics. Lang took great care to design his sets—for both his interior and exterior scenes—in such a way that the sets themselves almost become characters in the films with nearly as much life and influence as the human characters.

In Lang's German films the sets are imposing, even grandiose. The sets seem to dwarf the people on them and make them appear less strong, more controlled by the fates. In *Destiny* the dominant image of the early part of the film is the wall that the girl sees in her imagination or dreams. The wall is immense and seemingly impenetrable. As she stands at its foot, she is tiny in comparison with it; it is as though Lang is using the wall as a metaphor for her fate, which is also larger than she is and will dominate her life in the same way the wall dominates and towers over her.

In the opening of *Siegfried* Lang uses the set to indicate much the same message. When we first see Siegfried, he is at the forge shaping his sword. He is contrasted with the other people he is associated with; he is very white and blond and he is half naked, while the others are darker and clothed in shaggy, but full, dress. As he leaves the forge, he moves into a towering forest, which Lang created in the studio. He stands in beautiful contrast with the gigantic trees; but as powerful and distinctive as he is, he is dwarfed by the trees. Lang has used the forest to suggest to the viewer that no matter how much this hero may stand out from his environment, he is still only human and subject to a power greater than himself.

In *Metropolis* Lang used the city to represent the two sides of a struggle. The upper city, closely resembling the Garden of Eden, is the home of the managerial class while the city beneath the ground is the home of the workers. The area in between is the location of the industrial plant. The sets are all huge and impersonal, but the most striking is that of the exterior city above the ground. In her novel based on this screenplay, Thea von Harbou said that the main structure in this metropolis was known as "The New Tower of Babel," creating a direct relationship between the structure and the myth that is at the basis of the sermon Maria preaches to the workers. This set was inspired by the New York City skyline, with the biblical myth making a cautioning comment on modern society. The sets seem to dominate the film. The early advertisement for the movie in the *New York Times* features an even more stylized drawing of the skyscape in the film, and the ad copy emphasizes the sets rather than the plot: "Stupendous structures soar high in the air, Thunderous engines burrow deep in the earth. It's devouring! It's astounding!"[6] In fact, the sets so dominate the film that some critics believe that Lang allowed his interests in architecture to permit him to lose sight of the theme and plot of the film. *Times* critic Mordaunt Hall began his review: "If Fritz Lang, producer of the UFA picture 'Metropolis,' had given more thought to his story and less attention to the technical end of his production, he might have had a far more absorbing picture."[7]

When Lang left Germany and began to make pictures in the United States, his emphasis upon architecture shifted. As he got farther away from the expressionistic style that influenced his early films, he tended to construct sets that were less impressionistic and more realistic. He was also influenced in this country by the studio system, which gave him less time and money for his films; he was forced to cut back on the size and type of sets he used. As a result he did not build the gigantic sets he had used earlier, but he nevertheless continued to select his sets carefully, still fully aware of their symbolic, metaphoric, and thematic importance. The changing tastes of the public played an important role in his choice of sets, and so he began to photograph more realistic rooms and buildings. His old architect's eye, however, aided him in finding the right details to suggest the mood he wanted. The jail in *Fury* and the prison in *You Only Live Once*, the subway station in *Man Hunt*, the prostitute's apartment in *Woman in the Window*, the police station in *The Big Heat* and the newspaper city room in *While the City Sleeps*—these and many more sets reflect Lang's care for architectural detail and his awareness that the set can properly define his characters.

B. Geometrical Design

Lang's eye for architectural detail carried over into the design of his interior sets and the arrangement of his actors within the set, what the French call *mise-en-scène*. Lang was very fond of setting up a key scene with geometrical precision, balancing one side of the screen with the other or putting the object of chief interest in the exact middle of the screen, forcing the viewer's eye to the point of emphasis. Lotte Eisner calls this effect "geometrical stylization" and believes that it was "the last vestige of expressionistic aestheticism."[8]

Early in *Destiny* the image of the gigantic wall dominates the film. The first time we see it it covers the screen and dwarfs the girl at its bottom, roughly halfway between the sides of the screen. A few moments later the girl hallucinates and sees the wall again. This time there is a triangular door in the middle of it through which she passes very slowly to meet the death figure on the other side. In the first of these scenes, the geometric design of the wall and her relationship to it have emphasized the largeness of the wall and her smallness at its foot. In the second of the scenes, the stylization forces the viewer's eye to the break in the wall and to her efforts to penetrate it. The contrasts between the two scenes help to complete a metaphor about death and the unknown.

Geometric design can be used differently. Rather than creating the geometry through the relationship of actors and the set, it is possible to create design with actors alone. In *Clash by Night* one of the most moving scenes is the one in which the aging, but kind, Jerry finally realizes that his wife is having an affair with another man, Earl. While Mae is out with Earl, Jerry finds the presents Earl has given her and begins to realize the truth. Suddenly Mae and Earl return home and for a moment try to carry on their fiction, but Mae tires of the pretense, gives it up, and admits the truth. At this moment Lang fills the screen with the three characters. Earl is on one side of the screen and Jerry on the other. Mae is in the middle and a little behind the two men, so that they are in the forefront. Lang is saying visually what the dialogue is telling us aurally—that the confrontation is between the two men over this woman, who is caught between them and pulled toward both of them for different reasons. A few seconds later Mae makes her decision and goes to Earl. At this point the perfect geometrical design breaks down. No longer are the characters perfectly balanced; Mae goes and stands beside Earl. The lack of balance shows us that the decision has been made and that Jerry is now alone.

The ending of *Siegfried* makes consistent thematic use of geometrical design as Lang found ways to integrate design and theme in scenes that startle the viewer with their beauty. In one of them Lang wants to record the moment at which Kriemhild sees Siegfried's dead body for the first time. This scene is doubly important because not only has the love of these two been the chief theme of this film, but the revenge she seeks for the death of her lover is the chief theme of the sequel: this scene is the climax of the first film and the justification for the second. Lang dresses Kriemhild in white and the others in darker clothing, but it is the set and the location of the characters in it that draw the attention to this woman, who is to suffer so much and to cause so much suffering in others. The ceiling of the room has exposed beams that become part of the perspective

Siegfried: Kriemhild grieves for her husband

of the shot. The angles of the beams pull the eye into the center of the set where Kriemhild stands with Siegfried's body placed perpendicularly at her feet. After the camera establishes her grief and her opposition with the rest of her family that gather about her, the scene changes to the chapel in which we had seen Kriemhild praying in the opening scene of the film. She is with the body of her husband at the foot of the altar. The set is perfectly balanced, with candles and witnesses standing on each side of the woman. In this case the candles and witnesses pull the eye of the viewer into the group at the center of the set. The scene is lovely in the horror and sadness it creates, and it gives the entire film a sense of geometrical design in that it balances perfectly with the lovely scene which opened the film.

Lang's use of geometrical design must have appealed to his aesthetic sense, developed through the study of architecture and through his work in the graphic arts as a young man. This design gives to his films moments of breathtaking beauty, but it has more value than aesthetics alone. Lang has discovered ways to unite the design with the theme in order to present the theme visually and aesthetically.

C. Mirrors

Lang's use of mirrors indicates his attention to detail and his ability to make use of even the smallest part of the set in order to tell his story. Mirrors, or any other type of reflection in water or windows for instance, appear in almost every Lang film. Sometimes they are not especially important, as when a woman combs her hair or a man straightens his tie; sometimes the mirrors reflect the chief character at a moment of stress, as in *M* when the shop window reflects the murderer just before he strikes again. Sometimes the mirrors become a symbol for an unseen action, as in *The Blue Gardenia* when Norah breaks the mirror through which we have followed the action just as she hits Harry with a fireplace poker.

Nowhere is the mirror more important to the action and the theme than in *The Big Heat*. Just before Vince throws the coffee in Debbie's face, we watch her brush her hair before a mirror. The mirror serves a double purpose. First it emphasizes Debbie's vanity, but the mirror also serves to heighten the beauty of her face which is about to be ruined with the hot coffee. Not only do we see the face once; we see it twice. Vanity, beauty, and horror are all combined in the one shot of Debbie and the mirror.

In his last film Lang also made unusual use of a mirror. In *The Thousand Eyes of Dr. Mabuse* a two-way mirror is used by Henry Travers to spy on his girl friend in her hotel room (in the days of heavy censorship restrictions Lang often found ways to suggest a hint of voyeurism). Later he breaks through this mirror like Batman in order to rescue Marion from a man he believes is about to assault her.

The mirrors illustrate Lang's attention to detail and his awareness of means of making the set part of his statement on theme. Something as ordinary as a mirror, a puddle, or a window can be used to reflect the action and emphasize the object or character Lang wants to highlight.

D. Dress

One of Lang's most common methods of expressing the inner struggles that engage his characters is through their dress. Generally his technique is to begin the film with his character well dressed; then as the struggle affects him and he becomes depressed or degenerate, the dress also deteriorates. Finally if he rises above the struggle and conquers the odds against him, his dress is restored.

This practice in Lang's films is so often evident that numerous cases need not be cited, but the dress of Joe Wilson in *Fury* may be used as an example. When we first see Joe he is standing on the street with his girl, looking into a store window. He is neatly dressed in a topcoat and hat. Under the coat is a tie. There is nothing expensive about his dress, but it is nice. Later after his escape from the fiery jail, his appearance deteriorates along with his mental and moral attitudes. As he sits drinking in the hotel room waiting for the outcome of the trial, he is disheveled. His hair is unkempt, his shirt is partly unbuttoned and is wrinkled, and his jacket needs pressing. Then the next day when he appears in front of the judge, his dress is completely done over to match his new moral outlook. On this day he is impeccably attired in a neat three-piece wool suit, with white shirt and coordinating tie; his clothes would have been in perfect keeping at a wedding or a church service. In the same scene, not accidentally, the defendants, whom he has saved by appearing, are by contrast with Joe disheveled and unkempt.

Fury: Joe as degenerated man and as rejuvenated man

German Expressionism

For editorial reasons it is not the purpose of this book to dwell upon German Expressionism and its influence on Fritz Lang, but since that influence was pervasive, some acknowledgment of its role in shaping his techniques must be made.

Some of his early films such as *Destiny* and the Nibelungen Saga were made during the Expressionistic movement and demonstrate the movement as well as does *The Cabinet of Dr. Caligari*. With the films Lang made in the thirties, however, he began to move away from expressionism; and by the time he began making movies in the United States, he was demonstrating other influences.

Some of the characteristics of Expressionism, however, were to become such an integral part of his style that they remained with him even long after the movement was no longer dominant. Of these it is surprising how many continued to characterize Lang's films throughout his career: the use of shadows and light in sharp contrast, the obsession with corridors and stairways, the fascination with mirrors both as symbol and decoration, the construction of geometric sets, and the handling of crowds. Many of these techniques and devices discussed earlier in this chapter are therefore remnants of Lang's early infatuation with Expressionism.

4

The Nibelungen Saga

PERHAPS NONE OF LANG'S FILMS illustrates his use of the dark struggle better than his Nibelungen Saga. Fate, both exterior and interior conflicts, character degeneration—all are important to Lang's version of ancient German myth. Actually there are two films—*Siegfried* and *Kriemhild's Revenge*—which compose the Saga. Each is feature length, but they were intended to be shown as a unit and neither is complete without the other. Unfortunately the American opening of *Kriemhild's Revenge* was held up for three years after the opening of *Siegfried,* and the two have been rarely shown together in this country. In this chapter, where appropriate, they will be discussed as a unit.

Germanic Myth

The legend of Siegfried and his wife is familiar, and Lang worked within the traditions in order to treat his viewers to a cinematic version of the legend. Siegfried hears of the beauty of Kriemhild and rides off to court her. On the way he defeats a dragon and bathes in its blood, making himself invulnerable except at the spot on his back where a falling leaf prevents the blood from soaking his skin. He also captures the treasure of the Nibelungens by defeating its dwarf owners, taking in addition a magic cloak that will make a person disappear. He wins Kriemhild's hand but before the marriage he has to help her brother, Gunther, win Brunhild, the woman of his choice. She is athletic, and her suitors have to defeat her in battle before she will submit. With the help of Siegfried—hidden by the magic cloak—Gunther defeats Brunhild. Both men marry their women, but animosity develops between the women and reaches a point when Kriemhild reveals to Brunhild that Siegfried had been involved in her defeat. Brunhild swears revenge and convinces Gunther's loyal vassal, Hagan, to help. He dupes Kriemhild into

65

revealing the vulnerable spot on Siegfried's back and takes the first
opportunity to put a spear through it. Kriemhild's grief is as deep
and anguished as it is sudden. She knows that Hagan is the guilty
man when Siegfried's wounds begin to bleed in the presence of the
killer. (The scene describing this old folktale is unfortunately missing from one of the versions of the film being circulated in this
country). Calmly she plots her actions. She marries Attila the Hun
and moves to his country. At first chance, she invites her brother
and Hagan to visit her. Once there she entertains them at a banquet, surprises them, and through one means or another slaughters
the entire group. She is then killed by one of her own vassals; Attila
orders that she be sent home and buried next to Siegfried, since she
never really belonged to another man.

The scale of the filmed saga is immense. No costs were spared in
the production, which was in a grand manner seldom permitted
since. Lang's studio, UFA, operated what was considered the
largest facility in the world near Berlin, and he took full advantage of
his resources. Unable to control the elements outdoors, Lang
created an interior set that permitted construction of a larger-than-
life forest and perfect weather, fog on demand, and a seventy-foot
dragon. The saga was about two years in production, and Lang
allowed himself fifteen weeks to shoot *Siegfried* and sixteen for
Kriemhild's Revenge, roughly twice as long as he had to shoot most
of his American films. Later Hugo Riesenfeld was commissioned to
put together a musical score based on Wagner which was played by
a symphonic orchestra of sixty musicians at the New York opening.

It was generally assumed in the United States at the time that the
film was based on Wagner's operas *Der Ring des Nibelungen*, the
ring triology. Mordaunt Hall based almost his entire review in the
New York Times on the concept that Lang had been trying to film an
opera.[1] But in fact Lang and Thea von Harbou, who got sole credit
for the screenplay, resorted to different sources. Jensen makes a
strong argument for their having used a nineteenth-century drama
by Friedrich Hebbel called *Die Nibelungen*. Hebbel had divided his
drama into two parts and had simplified the roles of some of the
characters in order to give better dramatic unity. Jensen believes
that the screenwriters were familiar with this drama but felt free to
ignore Hebbel's strong religious interpretations of the original
myths.[2]

But, of course, Lang and von Harbou also were familiar with the epic poem *The Nibelungenlied*, also one of Hebbel's sources. An anonymous Austrian poet early in the thirteenth century wrote down his version of the legends of the death of Siegfried and his wife's revenge on his murderers. Compared to the other great epic poems, *The Nibelungenlied* has some weaknesses, but the strength of the characters and the horror of the actions give it vitality. The screenwriters also knew the Eddic folk songs and tales on which the epic poem was based because some of what they describe, especially Siegfried's training as a blacksmith, only hinted at in *The Nibelungenlied*, is described in detail in the other medieval sources.

Regardless of the specific sources used by Lang and von Harbou, it is clear that they were trying to capture the epic qualities of the Nibelungen legend: the formality, the pageantry, the heroic characters, the fierce action, the poetry. The word *epic* is all too often applied to motion pictures which try to explain in two hours of film how the West was won or how the battle of such and such was the turning point in some war, but Lang was seriously trying to emulate an epic poem in these films, and they are epic in more senses than simply scope of the subject matter. First, like the epic in literature, the Nibelungen Saga is a formal work of art. *Siegfried*, particularly, is formally structured and carefully paced. Early in the film we see the young, innocent Kriemhild at her prayers in the chapel. She is standing at an altar whose geometric design pulls the viewer's eye directly onto the figure of the worshipper. There is a formality to the church scene that is lent by the rigidness of the design and by the service, but the formality is heightened by Lang's repeating the scene at the end of the film. This time Kriemhild has returned to the church, but she is now there for the funeral of her husband. The set is almost exactly the same, but the body of Siegfried has been added. Thus the formality of what is being shot is furthered by the formality of the structure of the film.

Second, epic poems are also renowned for their pageantry. The poets describe in loving detail the pageants of court, love, war, and church, the Nibelungen poet no less than other epic poets. Lang has been able to translate this characteristic of the poem to film with ease (perhaps because film in general is a medium well suited for pageantry). He shows us the carefully paced procession as Siegfried enters Gunther's castle for the first time and the elaborate gestures and movements as Siegfried and Kriemhild greet each other for the first time. *Kriemhild's Revenge* is less formal and makes less use of

Siegfried: Top: Kriemhild visits the chapel in full sun light
Bottom: At the end, Kriemhild returns to the chapel to visit the body of
her husband

pageantry than does the first film, but as Jensen has explained, the subject of the second film is the description of the chaos that reigns during the revenge. Formality and pageantry are well suited for courtship and court games, but not well suited for the ferocity that results from a woman wronged.[3] This is evidence that Lang is not using formality and pageantry for their own sake, but to emphasize his theme. Unlike other "decorative"[4] films such as *El Cid* and *Cleopatra*, the Nibelungen Saga films use the epic characteristics to reflect the actions of the characters.

Third, these characters are heroic in a sense. Siegfried rises from an obscure blacksmith to the wealthy coequal of a king. His fame is widespread for his powers in battle and his success as a dragon slayer. He is handsome, blond; his presence illuminates a scene. Gunther, too, is a highly respected king who, while no match for Siegfried, is renowned in his own right.

There is the suggestion that the original poet intended their heroism to be considered ironically. As a hero Siegfried makes much of his reputation fighting dwarves, and he does not survive beyond the middle of the work. Gunther is hung on a hook by his wife on their wedding night. Lang seems to remove some of this irony, in part, by combining the three brothers of the poem into the single character Gunther.

Perhaps, however, the most interesting of the male heroes is Hagan. The first time we see him he is suspicious of Siegfried and jealous of his successes; certainly he does not seem to have the makings of a hero. He sinks even lower when he betrays Kriemhild and kills Siegfried, not *mano a mano*, but with a cowardly blow to the back. But in *Kriemhild's Revenge* he gains stature and becomes one of the heroes. As Kriemhild degenerates under the pressure for revenge, Hagan establishes his loyalty to his liege lord and proves his bravery, both in battle and in the fire. The man who dies at the end of the saga is a different man from the one who played the villain in the first part. In one sense he has not changed: he has always maintained a fierce sense of loyalty. But adversity builds character, and in Hagan it builds nobility.

The heroic demeanor of the women cannot be slighted. Brunhild is as much a champion at the games as is any man but Siegfried. She has bested all her suitors at the javelin, the shot, and the jump. Her pride in her powers is understandable, as is her anger at being duped by Siegfried. It is her uncontrollable rage at the insult to her pride that gives her the impetus to great and tragic action. Lang does make one change from his epic source in dealing with her. In the *Nibelungenlied* she seems to disappear after Siegfried's death, while in the film Kriemhild announces that Brunhild has died from a self-administered dose of poison. Kriemhild, like Hagan, is a major figure in both films in the saga. In the first of the films, she is a beautiful figure whose role is secondary to that of her husband. But after his death she dominates the second film, as she had the second part of the epic poem. At first she seems no more than the courtly lady of romances: demure, beautiful, subservient to her husband. But in the second film she develops into a character of heroic proportions suitable for an epic. She becomes a woman who determines her own future and who dominates the men about her. Her rage destroys almost everyone, both friend and foe. *The Nibelungenlied* was written late for an epic, and its poet was influenced by the medieval enthusiasm for romance, but the rage of Kriemhild lifts the poem from the level of romance to that of epic.

Fourth, epic literature is poetry, but unfortunately most Americans read the classical epics in prose translations. Lang, of course, knew the *Nibelungenlied* in its poetic form, and his movies are in part an attempt to capture the poetry of the original on film. Poetry and film are obviously two different media, but film can represent the rhythm, images, and language of poetry. Like the first part of the poem, *Siegfried*'s rhythm is slow and ponderous. Even the action of the games in which Siefried wins Brunhild for Gunther suggests slow motion because it is the beauty and significance of the action that Lang wants to portray. The pace of the second film recreates the furious rhythm of the second part of the poem as Kriemhild drives toward her revenge. The images of the poems are captured in the visual images of the film. For example, the Nibelungen poet describes in detail the first meeting between Siegfried and Kriemhild. He mentions the beauty of each of the lovers, the care with which they walk toward each other, the looks they exchange, the touching of their hands, and their growing love. Lang changes the circumstances somewhat, but the images of the details remain about the same. Lang has the two walk toward each other with deliberation and stare into each other's eyes, even as Siegfried drinks the wine she offers. Their hands touch briefly as he takes the goblet from her. Present in both poem and film is the image of powerful love about to spring forth. And finally the language is used similarly in both poem and film. Sometimes the writer of the title cards for the silent film tried to capture the epic language on his cards, and unfortunately the cards often seem stilted and awkward. More to the point, Lang tried to make his cinematic language correspond to the language of the poem. One of the most common uses of language is metaphor, and both poet and filmmaker use their languages to speak through metaphor. Both, for example, use the description of the dress of the characters to represent the morality of the characters. Kriemhild, in particular, changes from white to black as she becomes more obsessed with revenge.

Other epic characteristics appear in the films: the games, the emphasis on costumes, the descent into the underworld, the repetition of various scenes (at the beginning of *Kreimhild's Revenge* several of the scenes from *Siegfried* are repeated in order to orient the viewer in much the same way the epic poets repeated part of their poems for listeners who had forgotten where they left off), and the maintenance of the oral tradition (much of both poem and film is told by word of mouth or through song). No claim is made that Fritz Lang created an epic, since that is a poetic literary work, but the characteristics of his source that distinguish it from a romance or a

Siegfried: Kriemhild (in white) is challenged on the church steps by Brunhild

lyric poem have been preserved in such a manner as to distinguish the films from the rest of Lang's work.[5]

One of the characteristics of epic poetry is that each epic is usually associated with the development of a nation or race of people. Certainly the *Nibelungenlied* has been central to the myths of the German people, and Lang was consciously trying to create a cinematic version of that myth.

Just as each generation must write its own version of history, so each generation must give its own interpretation to the myth it inherits. Versions of the Nibelungen myths have been committed to song and verse for centuries, each varying somewhat from the earlier versions. The versions that dominated Germany in the early part of the twentieth century were those of Wagner and Hebbel, both written in the middle of the nineteenth century. Lang was obviously influenced by both of them (although his work is more closely related to Hebbel's than to Wagner's, in which Siegfried and Brunhild are the lovers and Kriemheld is omitted) and by the versions that were much older; but he, in using the myths from the past, was forced to give his own interpretation by virtue of the fact that he was of a new generation. Lang's view of this myth contains less religion than Hebbel's version and less mention of the struggles of the gods than Wagner's. He does not eschew all mention of religion, the gods, magic, or the supernatural because these elements are part of the tradition, but he does not give them the prominence they were awarded in their nineteenth-century sources. Instead he concentrates on the human exploits of his heroes. They are special people, capable of more than the rest of us mortals, but their powers are chiefly human ones. Siegfried is capable of putting on the magic cloak and disappearing, but the strength he displays while unseen to defeat Brunhild is his own. He is a superman, rather than a supernatural creature.

Kracauer believes that the climate that produced Lang's versions of German myth in 1924 was the same climate that produced the Nazi movement soon afterwards.[6] Perhaps, but the Nazis tended to use only the part of history they found to work to their advantage. While Lang was responding to the myths, the Nazis forced the myths to respond to them. In 1932 *Siegfried* was re-released by the Nazis with a Wagnerian soundtrack, but *Kriemhild's Revenge* was not released; it seems that some elements in Germany objected to the portrayal of Kriemhild as a degenerated woman.[7] Both Lang and the Nazis were shaping the myth to their own visions, but the visions were different and so were the purposes.

The Dark Struggle

At the heart of the epic myth is the struggle among and within the characters. Epics in general are characterized by gigantic conflicts between armies and supermen, and *The Nibelungenlied* is no exception. Lang includes the wars in the films, especially in part two; but he has concentrated on the struggles of his individuals. The struggle between Siegfried and Brunhild at the games gives the first film some of its best moments. Even the ultimate conflict between Hagan and Siegfried which results in the death of the latter begins as a footrace between them. In *Kriemhild's Revenge*, despite the fact that much of the film is consumed by the battle between Kriemhild's forces and those of her family (in one version I have seen, the fight takes up about 2700 feet of a film that is approximately 8,000 feet long—approximately 30 of 95 minutes—evidence that the fight dominates the film), Lang manages to bring out from the fighting masses the individual personalities of Hagan, Kriemhild, Rudiger, and Etzel. These people in conflict give the films their major theme.

Kracauer believes that the action of the film is controlled by Fate, which becomes manifest "through the anarchical outbursts of ungovernable instincts and passions. . . . An inherent necessity predetermines the disastrous sequence of love, hatred, jealousy and thirst for revenge."[8] On the surface this Fate is the classical fate that controls without concern the actions of characters. It is fate that directs the leaf that falls from the tree to land on Siegfried's back and make him vulnerable. It is fate that he discover the secret of the magic cloak and be in a position to assist Gunther with the conquering of Brunhild. But to limit the events of these films to the control of Fate is to misunderstand the extent to which Lang has his characters responsible for their own fates. Siegfried, perhaps, is doomed in an old-fashioned way, but he is responsible for revealing the secret of the wedding night when it should have remained untold. Kriemhild creates her own problems by bragging to Brunhild about the armlet Siegfried has given her and furthering the jealousy that already exists in this proud woman. Then Kriemhild seals Siegfried's fate by revealing to Hagan the vulnerable spot on Siegfried's back. This act is the seal on her fate, a fate that does not result from the uncontrollable actions of some force from the outside, but instead from the very controllable actions of the woman herself. This action leads to her grief, her rage, and her guilt—all three emotions contribute to the horror for which she is responsible in the concluding film. Her moral degeneration from one who loves to one who hates is accompanied by physical degeneration. The lovely young woman of the scene in which she first greets her lover turns into the frenetic, ugly creature urging her troops on to dreadful acts. Her face reflects her moral degeneration.

Hagan, too, is in control of his own fate. In *Siegfried* his actions are motivated by his loyalty to his king and queen; he is the perfect vassal. This loyalty leads him to heinous crimes which seal his fate. In all his actions he has free will and could make other choices, but he chooses deliberately the way that leads him step by step to the burning hall and Kriemhild's sword. Kracauer says that all of Hagan's loyalty is intended to mask a "nihilistic lust for power,"[9] but such a judgment fails to take into consideration the medieval sense of loyalty that was the source of this characterization. It seems that Kracauer was considering only the first part of Lang's saga because Hagan's nobility in the second part contradicts any claim of lust for power.

Visual Style

Perhaps in no other Lang film, not even *Metropolis*, did the various artistic temperaments of Germany in the 1920s combine to produce the startling unified effect of the saga. Lang's own interest in painting and architecture were the perfect complement for the talents of the designers he was fortunate enough to find: Otto Hunte, Erich Kettelhut, and Karl Vollbrecht. The characteristics of Expressionism meshed perfectly with the fairy-tale quality of the epic sources, and Lang's twentieth-century fatalism is expressed perfectly in the architectural design. Even though the architectural design is not expressionistic, the modernistic cleanness of its lines is a nice complement for the expressionistic scenes (for example, the forest and the fog) and acting.

The artists of Expressionism, regardless of their media, sought to express their feelings that man was controlled by his mechanistic environment. In the Nibelungen Saga, the mechanistic role is played not by a machine but by fate—a programmed universe. Lang uses a contemporary artistic concept to express the medieval concerns of his sources. Expressionism is well suited for the dark struggle in the Nibelungen Saga. First, Expressionism generally attempts to portray inner realities rather than exterior ones, a tendency easily used by Lang to depict the interior motives and degeneration of his characters. Second, Expressionism also deals with the larger question of man's role in the universe, his confusion, and his impotence—questions that fit neatly into Lang's theme. The result is that in the saga Lang has been able to fit his technique to his theme.

The UFA studio insisted that all movies be made in the studio so that the director would have complete control over the natural elements in his film. Lang needed a large, forbidding forest for his opening sequences of *Siegfried.* The trees were constructed on the set out of concrete; as a result Lang was able to use trees that were much larger than average. The effect was twofold: first, the closeness and size of the trees give an eerie, frightening feeling that portends the dangers of the quest on which the hero is about to embark through the forest; second, the trees dwarf Siegfried, who in turn has dwarfed the other men about him. Paul Richter, playing Siegfried, stands tall and straight while the blacksmith Mime and other inhabitants of the forest caves have been stooped. But even Siegfried is miniature in comparison with the forest. This extreme contrast between man and nature is visually unrealistic, but quite suitable for Lang's purposes. Later we will come to understand that Siegfried's fate will dwarf him in a similar manner.

Other scenes show Lang's drawing upon Expressionist techniques: Siegfried's ride through the fog and his fight with the king of the dwarves, his first view of the Nibelungen treasure, the passage of the Burgundanians through the fiery rocks that protect Brunhild. Each has the effect of increasing the fairy-tale atmosphere of the first part of the saga, but as indicated above, as Kriemhild seeks her revenge, the work becomes less of a romance and more of an epic. The second part of the filmed saga is less expressionistic and more realistic. The design of the sets is realistic, fewer symbols are employed, and the acting is less stylized. The horrors of fratricide and revenge are drawn from the reality of this world.

Even though it is not expressionistic, the contrary style of the geometric design of the architecture in its own way serves much the same purposes as the Expressionist devices. Lang made good use of "symmetrical and contrapuntal arrangements," to use Lotte Eisner's language. By perfectly balancing his characters within the huge sets he is able at the same time to dwarf them and to pull the viewer's eye in toward them as the axis of the symmetry. Many critics have commented on the effect of the view Lang gives us of Siegfried and his vassals waiting on the drawbridge before entering Gunther's castle, but the view of Kriemhild and Brunhild and their processions going up the steep church steps, each trying to be the first to enter for the services, is just as effective. The two women are dwarfed by the size of the steps and the church in the background, but the angles of their motion symbolize the inevitable conflict that is about to take place.

As Eisner points out, the effect of the massive and structured geometric design is to dehumanize the extras in the films. The footsoldiers become decorations within the castle or bobbing helmets as part of the bridge for Brunhild as she disembarks from the boat that has brought her to Gunther's castle. Only the main characters are personalized, forcing our attention upon them.[10]

The physical design of the film is reinforced by the special effects. Most often the special effects support the expressionistic side of the films and were for their day quite advanced and imaginative. The fogs that surround Siegfried as he rides through the forest were both important and difficult to produce. The chief problem was to allow the fogs to appear prominent without obscuring Siegfried and his white horse. A special chemical process, lighting placed behind the fog, and an especially dark night for photography combined to create this remarkable scene. And of course the dragon was the result of a major effort. This seventy-foot creature of plaster and rubber was animated by the movements of ten men hidden both within its body and in a pit under the body. Coordinating the movements of the dragon with those of Siegfried and the falling of the leaf from the tree took considerable time and energy on the part of the crew. The results were excellent for the twenties, but the dragon is now a bit dated by computerized apes and sharks.[11]

5

Dr. Mabuse

THE DR. MABUSE FILMS testify to Lang's career-long fascination with the theme of the dark struggle. From a film made early in Lang's career to one made at the end of the German period to one made at the end of his career, the Mabuse films deal with the conflict between society and the criminal forces that try to rule it. The films are exciting crime stories, full of psychological manipulation, suspense, and elaborate crimes. The films depict the efforts of Dr. Mabuse, a character taken from a well-known novel by Norbert Jacques, to dominate the world through various criminal means; yet they are more than the usual thrillers. Lang has managed to allow the films to become representatives of their age, to reflect the society in which they take place. The program notes released by the production company for the opening of the first of the films said, "Mankind, swept about and trampled down in the wake of war and revolution, takes revenge for years of anguish by indulging in lusts . . . and by passively or actively surrendering to crime."[1] This, then, reflects a larger struggle than that simply between Mabuse and his victims; it also demonstrates the constant struggle within society to maintain civilization and order.

The First Mabuse

The first of the three films was completed in 1922 and released through the German company Decla-Bioscop. Originally, the film was released in two parts, each of feature length and each seen on different evenings. The first part was called, in English, *Dr. Mabuse, the Great Gambler* and ran for about two hours;[2] the second part, of approximately the same length, was called *Inferno*. Since one must see both parts of the film in order to understand its thematic unity, they have been considered as a single film for the purpose of this study under a commonly accepted title, *Dr. Mabuse,*

Count Told in Dr. Mabuse, the Gambler

the Gambler. They have also been cut and released as a single feature film (in which Countess Told becomes the count's sister rather than his wife).

The central figure is Dr. Mabuse, the controlling and stabilizing element in a chaotic world, but his unique position is the result of his willpower over other people and his dream to rule the world for his own perverted reasons. During a wild party at which he is drinking with a group of men, for example, the doctor brags: "Now the world shall learn who I am—I Mabuse! I am going to be a giant—a titan who throws into turmoil laws and gods like so many autumn leaves." This thought establishes the character of the man that is to run throughout all three films and demonstrates that the real struggle here is between this force of evil and the laws of order that preserve society.

Lang believed that this film was a document of the age. He tried to find visual images to represent the degeneracy, confusion, and corruption rampant in post–World War I Germany. Through a series of short sequences during the opening part of *Dr. Mabuse,* Lang depicts the vice, murder, sex, gambling, and drugs that were characteristic of the Weimar Republic era. First, Mabuse is seen as a manipulator of the stock market. He has his people steal a contract important to the operation of a company; but after the market has dropped in reaction to the company's loss, he has the contract discovered, sending the market back up. Naturally he has bought when the market is low and sold when it is high.

Later Mabuse hypnotizes a young American, Edgar Hull, who then goes to a gambling club and loses a great deal of money to the disguised doctor. Hull also comes under the more personal influence of Mabuse's girl friend, Cara Carozza. When Hull tries to pay his gambling debt, he discovers another man in Mabuse's room, using the name of the man to whom he had lost his money. Naturally he is confused; but he meets a policeman, Norbert von Wenk, who is investigating the gambling clubs and who suspects that the two men Hull thinks he has met are in fact the same person. Wenk also is of the opinion that Cara is an accomplice. When the police raid one of the clubs, however, Mabuse uses the opportunity to have Hull killed. When the police arrest Cara, Mabuse, lonely for female attention, begins to seek a replacement.

His eyes focus on Countess Told, a pretty but bored woman unable to relate to the people about her, most especially her husband. The count himself is able to make few contributions to society. He is weak and of slight intelligence; his only passion is for his modern art collection. Mabuse hyponotizes the count and forces him to cheat at cards, an act which somehow brings some small moral fiber to light. He goes to Wenk, but he is so emotionally unstable that the prosecutor recommends him to Dr. Mabuse for psychiatric care, not knowing the evil nature of the doctor. Mabuse agrees to help the man because he is hungering after the countess and uses treatment as a means of getting the husband out of the way. Unbeknownst to the count, Mabuse captures the countess and holds her in Cara's room, hoping to seduce her through persuasion and fear rather than through rape. When the count comes to the doctor for counseling, Mabuse tells him that he will help only if he will agree to lock himself into his house and refuse until cured to see anyone who would remind him of his former life, not even his wife.

Meanwhile at the jail Police Inspector Wenk is visiting Cara Carozza, Mabuse's recently arrested mistress. He tells her to help herself by confessing what she knows about the murder of Hull. She asks for two days to think over his arguments and he leaves. As soon as she is alone, she says, "Blockhead," telling us she is loyal to Mabuse and is stalling for time with Wenk. Unfortunately for her, one of Mabuse's spies has heard all of her conversation with the policeman except the final word. Later he reports to the master criminal that Cara is untrustworthy, and Mabuse orders her death, giving the man a vial to take to Cara. The man returns to the jail and delivers the vial to the woman, who protests that she has done nothing to make Mabuse suspect her; but she takes the vial and drinks the poison as ordered, attesting to the immense power this evil man has over people.

In the meantime another of Mabuse's gang has taken a bomb to Wenk's office; the man, however, is surprised at his task and captured. In an effort to get him to confess, Wenk takes him to see the body of Cara as an example of Mabuse's treatment of his people. The man refuses to talk, but is soon assassinated by Mabuse anyway.

Mabuse goes to the countess and asks her to run away with him. When she refuses, the doctor tells her that he will remove all the obstacles between them, meaning her husband. During this conversation, Lang has crosscut to the count's house and shown him drunk and alone. It is clear that the treatment is increasing his illness rather than curing it. Lang shows us the count's mental deterioration through a marvelous scene of hallucination. As the count wanders through his house holding a large candelabrum, he sees the phantom of a man, probably Mabuse, who is holding a deck of cards. The man cuts the deck and shows the ace of hearts. More figures appear; they cut the cards and each gets the same card. The count runs from them and falls exhausted. The next day Mabuse comes and tells the count that since his illness has increased, his wife is going to have him committed to an asylum. Mabuse tells him, "Your life is ruined. . . . You cannot go on living." Mabuse leaves and the servant goes in to discover the count dead; he calls Wenk.

When Wenk interviews the man he thinks to be the count's psychoanalyst, they discuss the case of the dead count and the doctor tells the policeman that the count was under the influence of some overpowering and hostile mind. He then asks Wenk if he knows the work of Weltmann, a man who claims to be able to make people do the unnatural through the use of hypnosis, and Wenk decides to visit a public demonstration of the man's experiments.

As the scene shifts, we discover Mabuse putting on the makeup of Weltmann for the show. Lang has used mistaken identity to build up the suspense of the film; we have seen Mabuse as a respected doctor, a master criminal, and now as a magician. Once the demonstration begins, Weltmann/Mabuse is able to entice the policeman up on the stage to take part in the experiment. Before he knows what is happening to him, Wenk is under the power of Mabuse and is hypnotized. Mabuse tells him to get in his car and drive away. Other police try to follow, but Wenk drives away as if he is led by some mysterious force, as he too hallucinates. His men rescue him just before his car goes over a cliff; and as he returns to his senses, he tells his men that Mabuse is to blame for all the things they have not understood, and they go to surround his house.

The criminals decide to defend themselves despite the overwhelming odds, again attesting to the surprising power Mabuse has over his followers. Wenk calls Mabuse and tells him not to fight the state. Mabuse's reply is that he is a state within the state and they have been at war for a long time. This concept seems to be Lang's statement about the struggle between society and the forces of evil.

Wenk calls out the army which decides on a quick attack of the house, and a pitched bloody battle results. Finally, when the soldiers use hand grenades to storm the building, Mabuse grabs the countess and tries to escape through a secret passage. She struggles and escapes from him; moments later she is rescued and sent to safety.

Mabuse has gone underground through the sewer. He comes up inside the criminal's counterfeiting workroom in another building, but he discovers all the doors locked and he cannot escape. He has deteriorated from the calm, smooth, well-dressed gentleman he portrayed for so much of the film. Now he is scared, defeated, disheveled. Now Mabuse, even Mabuse the master criminal who controlled so many people, begins to lose control of himself and to hallucinate. He fantasizes the ghosts of his victims, and frantic at the memory of his deeds, he collapses. When the police finally break in, he has cracked. He is sitting on the floor playing with counterfeit money like a child. Insane, he is carried off between two policemen, and the movie ends. His insanity brings the structure of the film full circle; it had begun with the insanity of Count Told.

The Last Will of Dr. Mabuse (1932)

In 1932 a producer went to Lang and asked for a sequel to the Mabuse film. Lang tells us that the person said to him, "Look, Mr. Lang, we have made so much money with *Mabuse*," and he quickly

Dr. Baum, the psychiatrist controlled by Mabuse, lectures in *The Last Will of Dr. Mabuse.*

replied, "Yes, much more than I did."[3] But Lang was intrigued with the possibility of using the Mabuse theme again. The doctor had been left insane at the end of the first film. The problem was how to bring him back. Lang made use of the power over his followers Lang had developed for Mabuse in the first film. For the second film, *The Last Will of Dr. Mabuse*, Lang maintained Mabuse's insanity but had him come to control the mind of the psychiatrist who is treating the master criminal at the state hospital. Through the mind of this second doctor, Mabuse continues to rule the underworld. Lang may also have sensed that Dr. Mabuse gave him a vehicle for attacking the emerging Nazi party.

The film opens with one of Lang's best sequences. The camera reveals a frightened man hiding in a cellar. We do not know what he is hiding from or why the other men are there, but we sense that he is the man in whom we should place our sympathies and that the two men are trying to do him harm. They sense his presence and leave. Quietly and quickly he leaves. As he moves on to the street, an object falling from the top of a neighboring building narrowly misses him. Then suddenly men block his path and push a large steel drum at him. It explodes and nearly kills him. We have no explanation of all this action; it sets a tone of mystery, fear, and persecution that establishes the atmosphere for the entire film.

In the next sequence Inspector Lohmann (played by Otto Wernicke, creating the same role he played in *M*, Lang's previous film) is preparing to leave the police station. He says that "murder is taking a holiday" and there is no reason why he should not go to the fights. Just then the phone rings and Lohmann reluctantly agrees to talk with the caller, a former policeman who has taken to drink. The man says he can name the mastermind of the crime wave, but just as he is about to mouth the name, he sees something that drives him insane. Again we do not know what the source of the fear is, but we recognize the man as the one who so nearly missed being killed in the opening sequence.

The next sequence is located in a lecture room of a teaching hospital where a psychiatrist is lecturing on the case of the master criminal Dr. Mabuse. He tells his audience that he is Mabuse's doctor and that even in his insane state Mabuse writes lucid notes about the future control of man by a superior race.

In the meantime, Lohmann has gone to the scene of the former cop's phone call and is searching the room for evidence of what happened. He discovers some strange scratches on a window pane. They make no sense to him, but they seem to have been scratched by a ring as a message. Lohmann orders that the pane be taken to the laboratory for investigation.

Back at the hospital we see Dr. Mabuse writing frantically. At the same time, another doctor enters the office of the psychiatrist who is treating Mabuse and accidentally uncovers the secret of Dr. Mabuse. The psychiatrist, Dr. Baum, calls to his men, and a car follows the doctor as he drives toward the police station. At an intersection the occupants of the second car begin to blow their horn, the noise of which drowns out the shot as they kill the man and leave him sitting in the middle of the traffic.

The scene shifts to the members of the criminal gang, who discuss their mysterious boss, who is hidden behind a curtain and is never seen. One gang member, Kent, has fallen in love and wants to quit the gang. He has a date with his girl, but receives a note from Mabuse telling him to be at a meeting that night.

The scene cuts to Lohmann, who visits the former policeman, who has been located and taken to the same psychiatric hospital as Mabuse. As Lohmann goes in, the man hallucinates. He sits in his cell, talking over an imaginary phone to the inspector; Lohmann is unable to get any information from him.

Next we attend the meeting of the criminals that evening. The mastermind controls the meeting from behind the curtain; the leaders of the gang stand before him. His voice berates some of the men for not doing their jobs and compliments others. He tells one of them that he is not working as part of the organization: "The individual has no being except insofar as he is part of the machine. The individual is nothing; the machine is everything."

The camera takes us next to the police lab where a technician is working on the pane of glass. He connects the scratches and reads *Mabuse*. The inspector remembers an old case dealing with that name and goes to look it up to discover that the man is held at the hospital. But when he calls there, he is told Mabuse has just died. When he goes to confirm the death, we see Mabuse on a cart under a white sheet. There is no mistake; Mabuse is dead. But at almost the same time, the crooks receive notes that there will be another meeting. Now we are not so sure who is dead.

Dr. Baum makes a speech over the body of Mabuse about the need for the superman. He says the dead man had the blueprint for conquering the world. Later while reading from Mabuse's notes, entitled, "Domination by Terror," Baum begins to hallucinate and thinks he sees Mabuse talking to him. Mabuse tells him that the time for action has come, and Mabuse's body takes over that of the doctor. The doctor goes to the room and gives the criminals their orders for robbery and counterfeiting, telling them that "failure will not be tolerated."

In the meantime Kent and Lilly, his girl, meet. He tells her what his problem is and that he cannot resign from the gang. They try to surrender to the police; but before they can, the gang captures them and takes them to the leader. The voice from behind the curtain sentences them to death. Kent shoots up the curtain, only to discover that there are only a speaker and a dummy behind it. The voice comes through the speaker and tells Kent that he has failed. When Kent and Lilly try to leave, they find that they are locked in the room with an explosive that is set to a timing device. They try to dig their way out through the wall, but find a steel plate behind it. Kent decides to try to use water from a line that runs through the room to deaden the explosive's force. The risk is that they will drown first or that the force will still be too powerful, but the alternative is sure death from the blast. They are lucky; the water does buffer the explosion and they escape to go to the police.

The suspense of this episode has been built by Lang's crosscutting between shots of the couple and shots of the police beginning to close in on the gang. After a fierce battle, several members of the gang are captured in an apartment. The last man in the rooms kills himself rather than surrender. Even in death the power of Dr. Mabuse is pervasive. From the evidence collected in the apartment and the interviews with the captured crooks, Lohmann begins to understand the crimes and to associate Baum with them. Then when Kent and Lilly arrive and accuse Mabuse of their attempted murder and of the crime wave, Lohmann decides to visit the hospital. There they break in only to find the doctor gone. They do discover a map of the criminal activity for the night and the time for the action and race frantically to the scene of the crime. There they spot Baum, but he escapes in his car with them in close pursuit. As mentioned earlier in Chapter 3, this scene is one of Lang's most interesting hallucinations. Baum's car seems to go faster and faster. The trees on the side of the road fly by and take on a particular white appearance. Dr. Mabuse appears at Baum's shoulder and whispers,

"Failed, failed." When Baum arrives at his hospital, he goes to his office, where he is met by Dr. Mabuse, who again tells him, "You failed." And at that time Baum's face becomes that of Mabuse. Mabuse has now taken over Baum completely—mind, body, and appearance. Shortly later when Lohmann arrives at the hospital, he finds Baum/Mabuse in Mabuse's old cell insanely ripping up sheets of paper.

Lang tells us that he and Thea von Harbou used the film as an opportunity to put into the mouths of the criminals slogans that suggest the Nazi party, which was taking over at about this time.[4] The quotation cited above concerning the relationship of the individual to the organization is an example of the political implications of the film. In a preface to the New York opening of the film in 1943 Lang wrote that the movie could be seen as "an allegory to show Hitler's processes or terrorism. Slogans and doctrines of the Third Reich have been put into the mouths of criminals in the film. Thus I hoped to expose the masked Nazi theory of the necessity to deliberately destroy everything which is precious to a people. . . ."[5] The result was that the Nazis banned the film and refused to permit its showing. Lang was able to smuggle an uncut print to France and edit it there once he had escaped from Germany and Dr. Goebbels's offer to make films for the Nazis.

As Kracauer says, there is little doubt that the films reflect the theories of the Nazi party and Lang's prediction of Nazi behavior, but there remain today some unanswered questions. First, why was Goebbels so willing to offer Lang a job if he understood the anti-Nazi aspects of this film; and second, what was the working relationship between Lang and his wife on this film? When he left Germany, she remained and worked for the Nazis. If she had those political leanings all along, why did she permit her husband to put her name on political ideology that runs counter to hers? We probably will never know the answers, although guessing at them is entertaining.

The Thousand Eyes of Dr. Mabuse (1960)

In the late 1950s Lang returned to Germany and a man came to him and offered him the chance to remake the Nibelungen films. When Lang turned him down, the man told Lang he had the rights to Mabuse and wanted Lang to remake *The Last Will of Dr. Mabuse,* but again Lang refused to remake one of his own pictures.

The man then asked if it were possible to make a new Mabuse. Lang recounts his response: "Look, for me the sonobitch is dead. Buried." But the man talked him into it when Lang came to realize the potentials for updating the story using the new techniques. He had a point he wanted to make about society: "the danger [is] that our civilization can be blown up, and . . . on the rubble of our civilization some realm of crime could be built up."[6]

Like a good magician's act, *The Thousand Eyes of Dr. Mabuse* is full of misdirection (misdirection in magic is the magician's use of one hand to direct the audience's attention away from what the other hand is doing). There are many clues, hidden identities, and suspicious acts that are intended to confuse the viewers and to create suspense. More so than in the earlier Mabuse movies, it is difficult to figure out who is who and to tell the bad guys from the good guys. Misdirection is a characteristic of many Lang films, especially in his later career, but the technique is particularly pronounced in this last film.

The film opens with the murder of a television reporter, who is killed in his car by a secret new weapon that silently fires a needle dart so small the wound is difficult to find. During a police conference on the murder, one of the men connects this crime to a number of recent mysteries associated with the Hotel Luxor and says that he now has an agent there working undercover.

In the meantime, chief inspector Krass has received a phone call from a blind mystic, Cornelius, who said that he had seen the murder even though he had not been present. He tells Krass that this is a murder even before the police have found the needle and declared the reporter's death anything but a heart attack.

At about the same time back at the hotel, a woman is standing on the ledge, about to jump to her death. She is talked in by Henry Travers, who we discover is a high roller in international finance. Travers calls the woman's psychiatrist, Dr. Jordan, who comes at once and tells him that the woman, Marion Menil, has been in his care for some time. According to the doctor, Travers is the first person she seems to have trusted. Krass enters this crime also and investigates Marion. While in the hotel he has a drink with an insurance salesman, who asks too many questions and seems to have a questionable background. Confusion and paranoia begin to build.

Meanwhile, Travers, while riding in his limousine, almost hits Cornelius. To make up for what he thinks is carelessness, Travers offers Cornelius a ride. Once in the car, the clairvoyant predicts an accident, which the driver avoids only because of the warning. Travers is convinced that Cornelius is gifted; and when he predicts that one of Travers's business deals is going to turn sour, Travers is impressed.

Back at the police station Krass's office is bombed and he escapes only by chance. One of his aides is killed in his place.

When the camera returns to Travers, he is watching Marion sell some of her jewelry. He confronts her and gently interferes with her business. He is obviously fond of her and offers her an evening out on the town. She accepts and finally confesses that she is running away from an unhappy marriage. During dinner an aide interrupts the meal with a business matter. Because of Cornelius's earlier warning, Travers stops payment on a check that he has written to close a deal. Later we find that this action saved Travers's money because there was an explosion at the factory in which Travers had intended to invest.

At about this time in the film Lang introduced two devices that he needed to modernize the Mabuse myth. First, we see several scenes on a television monitor. Slowly we become aware that no matter where Travers goes in the hotel he is watched over closed-circuit televison. The thousand eyes of Dr. Mabuse are the television cameras subtly hidden throughout the building. Someone, we are not sure who, is watching everything Travers does. Second, one of the officers of the hotel tells Travers he can help him watch over Marion and shows him the two-way mirror discussed in Chapter 3.

Shortly afterwards, Krass, hoping to break the case, invites the principals to a seance set up by Cornelius. That night as they gather in a circle, Cornelius goes into his act. He discusses the murder of the reporter and mentions Dr. Mabuse. He speaks of danger just as a shot rings out, just missing Krass. After a fruitless chase after the would-be assassin, Krass comments to the other guests that this is the second time attempts recently have been made on his life. Cornelius reminds the inspector, however, that he, Cornelius, had been sitting in the chair seconds before he and Krass had exchanged seats, putting Krass in the line of fire. This is a good instance of misdirection of Lang's part. We cannot be sure if Cornelius is the victim or the mastermind.

Back in the hotel, Travers and Marion go to his room. When he asks her to marry him, she tells her story. Married to a cruel man who beat her, she tried to kill him but failed and has come to the hotel to escape him. At this moment, Dr. Jordan calls her to say that her husband is on his way to the hotel. She runs to her room in fright. Travers goes to the secret mirror to watch.

Her husband, a club-footed man who has been seen several times in the film when crimes have been committed, comes in and begins to attack her. Travers jumps through the mirror, picks up her gun from the floor, and shoots the man. The two lovers decide to cover up, and she calls Jordan to assist. When Jordan arrives, he pronounces the man dead and takes the body off in his ambulance. Once in the ambulance, the man we have supposed to be dead, sits up and says to the ambulance attendant, "Well, it worked just like the doctor said it would." At that moment the attendant kills the man. For the first time our suspicions that Jordan is mixed up in the criminal world are confirmed.

Back in the hotel, Travers suddenly realizes that he has been set up. He remembers that when Marion called Dr. Jordan about the murder, she used a three-digit phone number of some room within the hotel. She admits that she lied and points out to him the television camera, saying, "They see everything." When they try to escape, they are captured and taken to an air-raid vault in the basement of the hotel. There they see the television monitors and the entire system for spying on the hotel rooms. Jordan enters and brags about his plan. He says that Marion had been hypnotized to help him and that he wants the atomic factories Travers controls. He understands that he is either mad or a genius and credits the plan to Dr. Mabuse.

Now that the secrets are known to the audience, the rest of the film consists of the apprehension of the gang. First, the insurance man uses Cornelius's dog to expose Dr. Jordan as Cornelius, and we discover that the insurance man is an agent of Interpol. Then Krass and the rest of the police chase after Cornelius/Jordan, in cars and on motorcycles. Cornelius/Jordan pushes one of his men out of his car in an effort to slow up the pursurers, but finally he loses control of his car, crashes through the protective rail of a bridge, and sinks into the water.

In the final scene, Marion awakes in a hospital. Travers is beside her, and they kiss.

Like many last works of great artists, *The Thousand Eyes of Dr. Mabuse* is a summation of earlier works and derivative from that work. It is a good suspense story that forces the audience to remain intellectually alert through misdirected clues and mistaken identity, but somehow the movie lacks the life and creativity of Lang's earlier works. Many of the scenes Lang had used before: the explosion in the policeman's office was borrowed from *The Last Will of Dr. Mabuse*; the seance had been important in *Ministry of Fear*; and so on. The most imaginative creation in this film is the use of modern technology to make the crimes of Mabuse seem even more horrible.

The World of Dr. Mabuse: the Dark Struggle

Because the three Mabuse films span the long career of a director who always reflected the social milieu in which he worked, they can be considered as statements of the struggle between crime and society as Lang saw it at the time each film was made. In *Dr. Mabuse, the Gambler* the police are as unlikable as the crooks. Wenk, the policeman, bullies his informants and unhesitatingly uses the full violence of the army to root out the gang. Even Mabuse's primary victim, Count Told, is a compulsive gambler whose weakness drives him outside the law. Perhaps the only person for whom sympathy can be felt is the countess, who seems to be innocent of everything but being beautiful. The basic struggle here is between Mabuse and the police, but the society protected by the police appears to be little better than the world of the criminals. Both physical and psychological violence dominate the actions of both sides, but at least the argument can be made that the violence of the police is in response to the violence offered by the criminals and that it ultimately protects the one woman worth saving.

In *The Last Will of Dr. Mabuse* the opposite sides in the struggle are more clearly delineated. The Nazi slogans about the domination of the world clearly mark the criminals as foes of liberty, and in contrast the police seem more sympathetic. Lohmann, for example, seems genuinely concerned about the fate of the drunk policeman, even though he is disgusted by the man's waste of talent through drink. He also tries to get the cornered criminals to surrender rather than fight to their deaths. Kent and Lilly are more likeable people than the count and countess of the earlier movie. Kent's decision to leave the gang is better motivated than that of the count, and he is more likely to take positive steps to insure his freedom than was the complacent and pliable count. It is the Nazi slogans that ultimately establish the relationship between the film and its world. As John

Russell Taylor suggests, this ideology seems to be more a comment on the type of society that would or could nurture a Mabuse than it is a statement of the plans of a master criminal.[7] The Mabuse films are not blueprints for the takeover by supercriminals, but warnings that society needs to be alert to the intentions of such men or women.

Each of the Mabuse films makes use of the most sophisticated methods available to criminals at the time of the film. But the last of the three is in a philosophical sense the most frightening because it combines the psychological terror and the ruthlessness of the early films with the ability to control people technologically. The horror of controlling the minds of one's victims is intensified when the evil is used to try to obtain control of atomic-energy resources for personal gain, as in *The Thousand Eyes of Dr. Mabuse*. The abuse of atomic technology is frightening; but most people, however, have only a vague reaction to the possibility of its misuse. To many, the prospect of a television camera in every room to spy on every activity is even more frightening. This is a technological abuse we can easily understand. The thousand eyes in the Hotel Luxor create a form of persecution from which it is seemingly impossible to escape. No matter what you plan, no matter what you think, it seems that the unseen enemy will know your actions and anticipate you. How can one survive in a world in which every action is monitored? This technology adds a modern element to the Mabuse myth; but when combined with predictions from a mystic and a seance, technology and magic make a strange comment on the era of the film.

The Touches of the Director

The mark of Fritz Lang is seen in these films through the obvious plot and theme repetition. As should be clear, the theme of the dark struggle dominates these films in several different ways. First, there are the external struggles between the forces of evil and the representatives of good. Mabuse represents symbolically in all three films the monstrous side of human character that wishes to dominate ruthlessly the rest of mankind, and the films portray the attempts of society in general to resist this domination. This is the struggle of the police against the crooks. Second, the films depict the individual struggles of specific individuals to resist the evil forces that are trying to destroy them or psychologically dominate them. This is the struggle of Wenk against Mabuse, of Lohmann against Baum and

Mabuse, and of Krass and Travers against Jordan. This struggle is not allegorical or symbolic; it is the basic confrontation of man against man. Third, there are the inner struggles of people who try to resist the evil forces that are urging them to commit evil. This interior struggle is the individual's attempt to resist the psychological possession that Mabuse tries to take of the mind and ultimately the bodies of some of the characters. Perhaps the second of the films best represents this motif as the figures of Baum and Mabuse begin to merge during the course of the film. Once Mabuse is dead, he begins the process of taking over the being of Baum. At first he simply controls Baum's mind; then he begins to move into his body until at the end it is difficult for the viewer to distinguish between them. This inner struggle is represented in a different way by the count in the first film, by Kent in the second, and by Marion in the third. All of these people have been involved with the evil of Mabuse, but have decided to try to break out of the gang. The struggle in their cases is between their knowledge of what is right and their fear of reprisals from Mabuse.

Lang's touches are seen in other ways as well, however. The uses of hallucinations, of madness, of special lighting effects remind us of Lang's other work. Here, too, are the memorable scenes that somehow seem to capture the mood of the entire film, such as the view in the first film of Cara Carozza retreating into the corner of her cell to get away from the policeman, or the one of the former policeman going insane at the opening of the second film, or several in the third film of the television cameras monitoring the activities of the hotel.

And finally, Lang's control of his subject can be seen in the similarity of these films with *The Cabinet of Dr. Caligari*. Lang had made suggestions about the screenplay for that film thinking that he would direct it. In the end the studio took the film from Lang because he was wanted to direct a sequel to his successful *The Spiders*.

Lang did make some suggestions about *Caligari* that Robert Wiene used when he made the film, and Lang never lost his taste for the Caligari theme and incorporated parts of it into the Mabuse films. In these films there is heavy emphasis on psychology and insanity as there was in *Caligari*. Here, too, we are never sure who is insane and who is sane; here, too, we put trust in psychiatrists only to discover that they are not what we think them to be. Here, too, there is considerable use of dreams and visions. In general, Lang borrowed heavily from *Caligari* and continued to use motifs from the earlier project as long as he worked with the Mabuse theme. It should be remembered, however, that he was involved in the conception of *Caligari* and was only putting to use ideas that he might have wished to employ had he directed it. [8]

The three Mabuse films are a microcosmic view of Lang's major theme of the dark struggle. From the beginning to the end of his career he sought to portray man under pressure of evil. Each film may have been a reflection of its own time, but the theme underlying all three was universal and transcended the concerns of the particular years in which each was made.

6

The Films of Social Protest

IN THE 1930S, there was a cliché in Hollywood that expressed the opposition of many studios to message films: "If you want a message, go to Western Union." Some people in the film business thought that the primary use of film was entertainment and that to use film for didactic purposes was unaesthetic and, most important, unrewarding financially. Fritz Lang thought the cliché was a stupid expression because he liked to include a message in his films.[1] It gave the audience something to hold on to, something to talk about, maintaining, he believed, the interest in the film and bringing the people into the box office. His attitude suggests perhaps that his reasons for including social commentary in his films are more economic and commercial than humanistic, but in his films there is direct evidence that Lang's social conscience ran deep. His social themes are large, important, and contemporary: the treatment of a child murderer, the persecution of former criminals, the death penalty. But somehow Lang's concern for individuals penetrated the social positions of the films; the artistic emphasis is on the dark struggles of the individuals who encounter the social problem rather than on the social problem itself.

In subtle ways Fritz Lang was probably a maker of social-protest films from the beginning. Even a film as early as *Destiny* suggests that some of the problems confronting the young girl are the result of the greed and lust for power in the people who interpret her fantasies. *Metropolis* becomes a visual representation of shallow social philosophy. Perhaps the weakest part of this important film is Lang's resolution of the conflict between the ruling class and the workers by having the heart mediate between the brain and the hands, an idea that Lotte Eisner attributes to Thea von Harbou and not to Lang. But nevertheless the social protest is there. The Mabuse films contain commentary on both police and criminals, and

97

The murderer, Franz Becker, begs for his life at his trial

the anti-Nazi films are, of course, social protest against totalitarian governments.

Some of Lang's films, however, were created with a more avowed social purpose than these films. Among them are some of the best films Lang ever made, but there probably is no causal relationship between that fact and their social content.

M (1931)

The social climate of Germany at the time M was released is illustrated by a story told by Lang and recorded by Kracauer. The working title of the movie was Murderer Among Us; and when Lang went to a man he knew to ask permission to use a zeppelin barn as a set, the man became nervous and told Lang not to make the film. In his agitation, Lang grabbed the man by the lapel, felt a button, and realized the man was a member of the Nazi party. Suddenly Lang understood. The Nazis believed that the title referred to their leader and were trying to discourage its production. Lang assured them that the film was nonpolitical, and he shortened the title to the single letter.[2]

But while there may be suggestions of the Nazis in the film, its subject is quite something else. Lang and his wife decided to make a film about the worst crime they could imagine, the crime that is most likely to be rejected by the public. They tried several topics but none satisfied. Finally one day Lang went to von Harbou and suggested the subject of a child murderer "who is forced by a power within him to commit a crime which he afterwards resents very much."[3] There could be no darker struggle than that of a man who commits a heinous crime under the impulse of some inner force and has to struggle against himself. At the same time he struggles against the society that is trying to punish him for a crime over which he had no control.

Lang realized that the film could be viewed on several levels, depending on the audience. Some would see the film as a simple cops-and-robbers story; others would see it as the depiction of the manner in which the police go about their job; others would see the film as a commentary on the dangers faced by children in our society; and yet others would see it as a statement on capital punishment. Lang says that these last two interpretations are the main reasons he was interested in the story. Here is the social protest, which is perhaps why the film has remained Lang's favorite among all his work.[4]

The plot is not at all complicated. A small girl is killed, one of several such murders. When the police crack down on the criminal element in town in order to flush out the killer, the criminals band together to find the murderer, both because they too are appalled by his crimes and because they want the police to let up on them. The gangsters organize a careful search and a street-by-street plan for protecting young girls. The police also organize their search, which is less systematic than the criminals' and which relies heavily on the harrassment of the criminals. In the meantime the killer is ready to strike again. When he feels the compulsion to kill, he first expresses the need through a slightly off-key whistling of Grieg's "In the Hall of the Mountain King." He sights one girl but is put off when her mother appears. When he takes up with another girl, his whistling tips off a blind vendor who alerts the gang, and the chase is on. The killer escapes into a deserted office building and the gang begins to search it room by room. In the meantime the police have begun to make sense out of their clues, and they too are closing in on their man. The gang finds the man and spirits him away seconds before the police arrive at the office building. Taken to a large warehouse, the man is given a kangaroo trial by the criminals. At one point he breaks down and sobs, but shortly he regains his composure and defends himself, asking his accusers what they know about the type of crimes he has committed. He says that his accusers are criminals only because they are too lazy to work; but as for him, "I can't help myself! I haven't any control over this evil thing that's inside me—the fire, the voices, the torment."[5] The criminals show little sympathy or understanding, but before they can carry out their death threats, the police arrive and rescue the man.

The struggle in this plot is the most realistic of Lang's films up to this point; it is less allegorical than that of *Destiny*, the Nibelungen Saga, or *Metropolis*. It is less fantastical than that of *The Woman in the Moon* and much less oriented around the superman than the Mabuse films or *Spies*. Despite interesting exterior struggles, such as the one between the gang and the police to be the first to find the killer, the most poignant struggle is the internal one within Franz Becker, the killer. He is outwardly an ordinary man, quiet and a little shy. His life seems to be as simple as the plain room in which he lives. Yet on the inside Becker is a confused and frustrated man.

M: Franz Becker sees in a mirror the mark of the murderer

Visually the struggle is established in a series of scenes about mid-way in the film. First we see him, in a famous scene, standing on the street, eating an apple. He pauses in front of a store window displaying knives, and the reflection of the display creates a diamond-shaped pattern around him, a pattern that always reminds me of the bandoliers worn by Mexican bandits. As he stares into the window, suddenly the reflection of a small girl is mirrored beside him. He stares at her, and actor Peter Lorre's actions reveal his character's anguish. He wipes his mouth with the back of his hand; his already prominent eyes appear to bulge even farther. His arms fall limply to his sides, his breathing becomes uneven, and he shuts his eyes for a moment. When the girl walks off, he slowly follows, whistling his tune. Suddenly she greets a woman, and the whistling abruptly breaks off. Becker hides in a doorway, and the camera comes in close to show him nervously scratching his hand. The camera follows him into an outdoor café. We watch him through the leaves of a vine growing over a trellis. First he orders coffee, but quickly changes his mind and asks for vermouth, then even more quickly asks for something stronger. He drinks his brandy in a gulp, then takes another. He smokes a cigarette. He presses his balled fists to his face and begins to whistle again. He presses his hands over his ears, but suddenly he gets up, pays his bill, and leaves, whistling the Grieg theme. He has lost his struggle; the next time we see him he is buying sweets for a little girl. This statement of Becker's conflict has been accomplished visually with almost no dialogue. The acting of Lorre, the selection of the camera shots, and the whistling have told all.

Later at the end of the film the struggle becomes more verbal. During his "trial" Becker tries to escape but is stopped at the door. He falls in terror as the criminals laugh and demand his death. He bangs his head against the wall, a motion that reminds the audience of his mental and emotional unbalance. The camera comes in close on his face, showing the frenzy of a trapped man, trapped both within and without. As the shouts for his execution increase, he seems to grow in stature. He is still terrified, but he controls his frenzy. He stands up and confronts the gang. He denies their right to kill him, but then as the camera comes in again, he slowly sinks to his knees, sobbing over and over again, "I can't help it." He says that the evil force within him drives him to wander the streets: "It's me, pursuing myself." He says that he wants to escape; especially he wants to escape from himself. He runs through the streets: the images of the mothers of his victims haunt him. His only peace comes when he is with his victim, but later he cannot remember his acts. He comes to understand what he has done only by reading the wanted posters. At this point his defense becomes disjointed, almost stream-of-consciousness. His words suggest images rather than sentences. His voice does not complete his thoughts, but our imagination does. The leader of the gang says, "Someone who admits to being a compulsive murderer should be snuffed out, like a candle." Becker's drunken lawyer, however, has been impressed by the plea of his client. He refutes the leader with the claim that a man acting under compulsion is not responsible for his crimes and that society cannot punish a man not responsible. The crowd hoots its reply to such an idea, but the lawyer persists: " . . . This man is sick. And a sick man should be handed over, not to the executioner, but to the doctor." The mob responds with the familiar argument that a criminal committed to an asylum may someday again walk the streets. The cries for Becker's life rise again. This time the criminals become as frantic in their cries for his death as he had become in his defense: "Kill him, the beast. . . . Crush him, the brute. . . . Hang him."

Suddenly the police enter. The camera comes in to show the abject terror on Becker's face. A hand grasps him firmly on the shoulder and a voice says, "In the name of the law. . . ." There is no real resolution to Becker's struggle. There is no cure; one can easily imagine his torment. Little more can be said except that for a while he will not be running through the streets, driven by compulsion.

This struggle within the characters is reinforced through the cinematic techniques. Although less than a decade away from the Nibelungen Saga, Lang depended less on geometric design and more on the relation between his human subject and the natural scene in which he finds himself. Lang still used the concept of the anonymous mob, a holdover from Expressionism that would be used again in *Fury*; the individual is lost in large crowds shown in long shots or through quick pans. One of the most effective devices Lang used with the crowds is to show selected members of the mob in close-up but to use such short shots that the only impression on the eye of the viewer is of the frustrations that led to that person joining the mob. There can be no real sympathy on the part of the viewer for the persons shown because they are seen too briefly and without personality.

In many ways Lang's selection of shots for *M* can become a textbook for filmmakers. From long shots such as the one of the killer running through the streets to close-ups of Lorre's face as he cowers before his jury, Lang has a range of shots that almost perfectly match the narration.

No aspect of this film has been as much discussed as Lang's use of sound.[6] Since this is his first sound film and came early in the development of sound, his grasp of its use is remarkable. The whistled theme, the simplicity of the dialogue (when the killer makes his contact with his victim early in the film, the efficiency of the lines almost throws them away: "What a pretty ball. What's your name?"), the cry of a mother calling her missing daughter, echoing in an empty staircase well, the silence of the killer hiding—all these devices reveal the depth and terror of the struggles that are taking place.

The use of light is also particularly important in this film. As in Lang's earlier films, the chiaroscuro effects are especially important, but the artificiality of, say, the beam of light searching out Maria in Rotwang's cave is missing. The lights and shadows are more realistic in *M* than in the earlier films; Lang still uses light and shadows to highlight but he has begun to seek out natural light. In other words his use of chiaroscuro effects had become less allegorical. The Expressionist's love of shadows is still present, however, as for instance when the killer casts his shadow over the poster on which Elsie is bouncing her ball.

Perhaps the most subtle of Lang's techniques in the film is his sense of what must be suggested visually and what may be shown realistically. When Peter Bogdanovich asked Lang about not showing the actual violence in this film Lang replied at length about the aesthetics of violence. He told his interviewer that by not showing exactly what the killer did to Elsie he left it to the viewer's imagination. Each viewer will imagine for himself the most horrible thing the man could have done to the girl; for each viewer the imagined act will be different, an effect Lang could not have achieved by depicting all the details on the screen. Through this act each viewer participates in the crime and is thereby drawn into the film. The viewer comes to sympathize with the killer by having shared in his crime. All Lang shows of the act is Elsie's ball rolling from under a bush and her floating balloon becoming entangled in power lines. Lang's film is terrifying as, for example, *Straw Dogs,* in which Sam Peckinpah leaves none of the violence to the imagination. In a Peckinpah film it is the image of the violence, such as the image of a mantrap being sprung over the head and neck of a victim, that sticks with you as you leave the theater; with a Lang film it is the feeling of terror that sticks with you.

Fury (1936)

Lang's first American film is still the most popular of those he made once he left Germany, and it is the most frequently analyzed of all his American films. MGM had brought Lang to this country to make movies but never gave him a chance until his contract of one year was about to run out. One of the executives in the studio, Eddie Mannix, gave Lang a four-page outline of a film then called *Mob Rule* with Barlett Cromack as a screenwriter, and Lang was back in the business of making movies.

As the film opens, Joe Wilson and his fiancée, Katherine, are looking at bedroom furniture in a store window. We discover that they are young, in love, and without the money to marry. She is leaving to take a job in another town so that they can both save. When he returns alone to his flat, we see Joe in stark contrast with his slightly shady and drunken brothers. He is the good man who is trying to make his place in American society by getting a job and marrying the girl of his dreams (an interesting image to have been created by a man so recently an immigrant to this country). Time passes quickly in the film and the intervening months are depicted to us through letters Joe writes Katherine. Finally he has made his money and is on the way to pick her up for the wedding. It is a drive of a couple of days; he spends the night at a campsite in the woods in a state of almost mythical innocence. The next day he is stopped at a roadblock and questioned in connection with a kidnapping; the only evidence that implicates Joe is that both the guilty man and Joe like salted peanuts and that Joe could not account for the night spent on the road. He is locked up in the local jail, and mob hysteria begins to control the people of the town. Rumors spread, fears build up, and the sense of excitement and fun stimulate some people to participate in actions they cannot control. The citizens of the town become a mob and demand that the sheriff surrender Joe to them. When they are rebuffed, they break into the jail and set fire to it on discovering that they cannot get Joe out. Katherine arrives on the scene just in time to see Joe's face at the window of the enflamed building. As the national guard arrives too late to help, the crowd disperses. Unnoticed by the crowd, newsreel cameramen have photographed the entire escapade. Suddenly the frantic pace of the film stops. The crosscutting from Joe to the mob to Katherine has created a fast rhythm; that and the horror of watching a panicked man caught in a burning building have left the viewer breathless, but the film is not over.

In a transition scene the governor and a political boss read the headlines that proclaim that the kidnappers have been caught and an innocent man burned alive. The scene changes to Joe's gas station, where his brothers are reading the same headlines in a Chicago newspaper, making threatening noises which border on bluster. Suddenly a cold voice from the shadows tells them that their talk is "five and ten cent store" conversation. Joe appears in silhouette, almost ghostlike. He mutters in a scratchy voice. "Pull down the shades." He is now a man of darkness. The change in him is much like the one in Kriemhild between the two parts of the Nibelungen Saga. Both emerge from their torment with a sense of tragedy and a need for revenge. Joe plots his revenge on the people of Sage. He will remain "dead" and make sure they are tried and executed for his murder. In order to help the district attorney find a witness who will testify about what actually happened at the lynching, the brothers go to Katherine, whom they find in an almost catatonic state. She is unable to respond to their presence until one of the men begins to light a cigarette. Lang shows the reaction of her mind through a flashback to the scene of Joe at the window amidst the flames. One flame has awakened in her mind the image of the other. The shock brings her back to reality, and the brothers have their witness. Separately, of course, Joe and Katherine talk about their reasons for wanting to pursue the trial. Joe wants revenge and Katherine wants the wives of the men involved to feel the loss of a loved one. The distinction between revenge and retribution is a subtle one, but Lang uses that subtlety to make a statement about society's treatment of the criminal.

At the trial the DA first calls a series of witnesses who try to prove that all the defendants have alibis. He uses the newsfilm to prove dramatically the presence of the accused at the jail at the time of the fire (at the time Lang's use of newsfilm was imaginative; now of course it is common). The DA has demonstrated perjury, but not murder; when Katherine is called, she cannot prove that she knows that Joe died in the fire. The body has naturally never been located. The defense attorney claims that the prosecution has not proven that any murder took place. Joe, listening to the trial by radio, decides to take action. He sends the ring Katherine gave him in an anonymous letter to the judge with the claim that it was found in the ruins of the jail. The ring and its accompanying letter are submitted by the judge as evidence of the death of an innocent victim of the lynching. Katherine however, notices a misspelling in the letter that is characteristic of Joe; then she realizes that one of the brothers is wearing Joe's overcoat. She follows the brothers to confront Joe. In one of Lang's better scenes, she repudiates Joe; he tries to run away, but his conscience forces him to hallucinate. Through his mental anguish, he comes to understand his guilt for his sin and the next morning he appears dramatically in court and confesses. In a climactic speech before the court Joe explains his actions. He says that the men and women before the court are murderers and the fact that he is alive is not due to their effort. He tells the court that "silly things like a belief in justice, and an idea that men were civilized, and a feeling of pride that this country of mine was different from all others" have died within him. This is the source of his degeneracy during the latter part of the film. But he goes on to say that he did not want to live the rest of his life alone; he had been isolated by his actions and had lost Katherine. He says that he came back because that was the only way he could go on living.

It was at this point that Lang wanted to end the film. This speech is a good one, and the final point seems an honest one to make. The studio insisted, however, that Lang add a final kiss in the courtroom between Joe and Katherine. Lang argued that a kiss before the judge, the court, and all the people was anticlimactic and unnecessary; the studio persisted in its demands. He was right, but the studio won.[7]

Most of the reviewers of the film at the time it came out and most of its critics today discuss it as a lynching film, and with good reason. The mob scenes are frightening and visually memorable; they are among the outstanding scenes of American cinema. But I perceive the film to be more than a lynching film, one of several in that genre. The lynching takes place at roughly the midpoint in the film. Something like half the film is devoted to events that take place after the "murder," and Lang's emphasis in this part of the film is not so much on the guilt of the murderers as it is on the dark struggle of Joe as he wrestles with his need for revenge and his guilt and isolation that result from his actions. While lynching is an issue here, it is the effect of the lynching on the participants that is the major theme of the film: Katherine wanting other women to suffer, the citizens of Sage perjuring themselves to escape at least the legal guilt, and Joe distorting his soul to find revenge. The struggle between Joe and the mob at the jail is visually an artistic *tour de force*, the conflict between the DA and the defendants and their lawyers amuses us and satisfies our sense of poetic justice; but it is the struggle within Joe that brings universality to the film. The social theme is important but the ultimate social statement is concerned with the individual's responsibility to himself and those he loves.

Lang was also interested in mob psychology. It was this interest that led him to expand the four-page outline given him by the studio, and my emphasis on the response of the individual should in no way be interpreted as neglect of mob violence as a theme. Lang told interviewers that he had been through four revolutions and had studied the struggles at the center of the violence that took place. He tells the story of once having seen violence begin in Paris when a crowd watched with amusement a man bumping his cane on the bars of a fence. Suddenly the man reached the end of the fence and then used his cane to break the window of a shop. This action turned the crowd into a mob that began a riot that had to be stopped by the police. Lang says that it all started with the comment, "Oh, let's have some fun," a line that is yelled out by a youth as the mob leaves the bar in *Fury*.[8]

The reception of the film in its day was curious. The studio was embarrassed by it and wanted little publicity, but the reception of the critics was so favorable the studio allowed it a modest run. Almost all the reviews were favorable. Frank S. Nugent in the *New York Times* claimed that *Fury* was the finest dramatic film of 1936, and the *Time* reviewer said that the courtroom scene set "an all-time high for legal realism on the screen."[9] Other critics praised the film and concentrated their appreciation on the mob scenes and the antilynching theme, but they felt that the second part of the film was not satisfying. Otis Ferguson's comment seems to summarize this position: "MGM's picture *Fury* is a powerful and documented piece of fiction about a lynching for half its length, and for the remaining half a desperate attempt to make love, lynching and the Hays Office come out even."[10] It is probably true that the pace of the second part of the film is much slower than that of the first, that the audience involvement is less after the incineration, and that some of the speeches in the courtroom tend toward bombast. But it is in the second part of the film that Lang's social message endures. Lynching is not the social problem in America it was in 1936, but mass guilt and revenge have become more important.

You Only Live Once (1937)

Lang's next film after *Fury* was *You Only Live Once*, another movie in which social criticism formed a major theme. Gavin Lambert has written that in *You Only Live Once* "there are again only three characters: the outcast hero, his girl friend, society."[11] As social protest, this film focuses on what it is that society does to a young ex-convict. In a strict sense, Lambert is right in reducing the bulk of the characters in the film to the general description "society" and in discussing the role of society in repressing this man. But in another sense, Lambert has oversimplified what Lang has done. Many of the characters who oppose Eddie are individualized to the extent that they stand out from the mob called society. In Lang's earlier films—the Nibelungen Saga and *Metropolis*, for example—

the forces that surround the heroes are anonymous; the individuals in the crowds do not stand out. But a device Lang has learned is to make the members of the crowd individual. The forces that oppose Eddie in *You Only Live Once* are not anonymous; they are individuals whose character traits are carefully delineated. The warden who has seen too much crime and too many men return to his facility, the motel keepers who have read too many police magazines and are scared to have a criminal in their motel, the owner of the truck company who is more interested in his poker game than in Eddie's problems—all these individuals, and more, represent society; and it is against their helplessness, their callousness, that Lang is protesting.

The film opens with shots that establish the happiness of Jo, the secretary for a lawyer. She is about to leave for her wedding and everyone is happy for her but apprehensive about the match she has made, a man about to be released from prison. The camera cuts to the prison and we follow Eddie as he makes his last walk through the yard. The warden and the chaplain bid him farewell. The warden admonishes Eddie to remain inside the law, and Eddie replies, "I will, if they'll let me." He says that the last time he was out people would not give him a chance; he suspects the same fate this time. At the gate of the prison, however, Jo is waiting and the two go off together. The scene shifts to the Valley Tavern Inn, where the couple is preparing to spend their honeymoon. Eddie and Jo linger over a lily pond and watch the frogs. This is an important scene for several reasons. First, it establishes a theme of the Garden of Eden in which there is beauty and goodness. Second, it gives Eddie a chance to talk about his past and gives us insights into why he has become a criminal. Third, his comment that when one frog dies, the other dies, too, establishes foreboding about the outcome of this film. Later, as the young couple share their first night together, the manager of the motel and his wife interrupt. This episode establishes, in what is almost a humorous manner, society's attitude toward the ex-convict. This scene sets up for us a more serious one later in which Eddie loses his job and is convicted of robbery primarily because he is a former criminal.

Next Eddie gets a job as a truck driver. Time passes and the couple decides to buy a house. The one they look at is overgrown and a bit rundown, but the idyllic quality of it is reminiscent of the garden at the Valley Tavern Inn. Because he has stayed too long at the house, Eddie is late with his truck; and the firm's owner uses the lateness as an excuse to fire Eddie. He goes on the road looking for work; and when he calls home, he finds that Jo has moved into the house and that they have house payments to make. He goes to his former boss to beg for his job, but to no avail.

The scene cuts to a sign for the Fifth National Bank. Eyes peep from the back window of a car during a heavy rain storm. An armored car pulls up, and a man well dressed and with his face covered with a gas mask emerges from the car and throws a bomb which incapacitates the guards. The man commandeers the truck and speeds off, leaving a hat in his car with Eddie's initials in the lining. The truck has an accident in the fog and rain and disappears into a gorge. In the next scene Eddie appears at their house to tell Jo that he is innocent. Lang here has, like the magician, used misdirection to lead us as viewers to the wrong conclusions. We have assumed that the man in the mask is Eddie. We have committed the same mistake that the people in the film commit; we have looked at the circumstantial evidence and declared Eddie guilty. Quickly though, our sympathies for him return when the police surround the house and he is taken prisoner. The story of his trial is told through newspaper headlines (several years later Orson Welles used the same device in *Citizen Kane*). He is found guilty; Jo begs forgiveness for asking him to surrender, but he rejects her.

When she visits him in prison, awaiting his execution, she tells him she will do anything to help him. He asks her to smuggle in a gun; she goes to a pawnshop (the shot of Jo before the shop window is strongly suggestive of the shot of the killer in *M* as he stares into the shop window). With the gun she tries to go back into the prison, but she is detected and stopped by the priest. Defeated in her effort to assuage her guilt, she asks the priest to tell Eddie that she has not forgotten the frogs.

In his cell Eddie is smuggled word that there is a gun hidden for him in the prison hospital and that he should invent a reason for going there. He cuts his wrist with the tin cup, passes out and is rushed to the infirmary. This scene has taken place in the condemned cell, which Lang has lighted for dramatic effect. The bars of the cell are reflected on the floor by a strong backlight. The shadows have a double purpose. First, they seem to spread the cell out so that everything seen becomes part of it. Symbolically the outside world is part of that cell. Second, the sight lines of the shadows pull the eyes of the audience into the cell.

At the news of the injury, the warden's only concern is that Eddie live so that he can be executed. The prison doctor assures him that Eddie will be all right and that the execution can go on as scheduled.

Eddie finds the gun and begins to escape with the doctor as hostage. The scene shifts to the living room of the warden's house, where the warden and his wife are entertaining a few friends. The warden's wife offers the observation that Eddie was born bad, and the priest disagrees and gives the standard Christian view of Eddie. The warden says that he hopes that Eddie will not be born again to live another life on this earth because "he's caused enough trouble in this world." Suddenly the telephone rings to inform the warden that Eddie is not through causing trouble. He has escaped, with the doctor as a hostage.

The priest tries to convince Eddie to give himself up and shows him that the warden has a wire that the real robber has been found in the submerged truck and that Eddie is pardoned. But the gun goes off and the priest is hit. In his dying moments he tells the warden to open the gate and Eddie runs out.

Jo is called by Eddie and the two meet in a railroad yard to begin a long attempt to escape. The story of two lovers on the lam is now a familiar subject for film (*They Live by Night, Bonnie and Clyde,* and *The Getaway*), but never has the genre been more poignant than in the Lang version. Jo is forced to become a criminal as the two of them steal for sustenance, but the image Lang creates is one of the world closing in on people who are basically innocent. They long only for peace and a chance to raise their baby. There is a symbolically significant scene in which their child is born in a rundown cabin (not unlike a stable). The rain and fog of the other scenes during the escape have been replaced by a soft mist; Eddie has some hand-picked wild flowers as a present for Jo. But all this is to end.

When they try to give the baby to a family, they are spotted by an alert motel manager and reported. The police (dressed in uniforms that strangely resemble the stereotype of the German police) stop the car. Jo is shot and Eddie tries to carry her toward the border and freedom. Jo tells him that she would do it all again just before she dies. Then Eddie too is hit by a shot. As he falls, the priest's voice tells him that the gates are open for him now. In death, Eddie's face, as shown in a close-up, is calm, handsome, glassy. The final shot is of the forest, full of sun and peace, a direct contrast with the rainy and foggy scenes of their frantic race to escape. The contrast is meaningful, but the apocalyptic vision creates a romantic conclusion that is hardly in keeping with the driving tone of the social commentary of the rest of the film. Robert Stebbins in *New Theatre* commented in his contemporary review that the film "was considerably marred by an unpleasant, mawkish last minute addition to the end . . ., probably through Hays Office insistence."[12]

Stebbins's review, in which he criticized the screenplay because of the weaknesses of plot but praised the direction, was typical of the critical reception of the film. Frank Nugent in the *New York Times* made the same points but with more vigor. Despite the limitations of the script, he wrote, the film is "an intense, absorbing and relentlessly pursued tragedy which owes most of its dignity to the eloquence of its direction." He goes on to commend Lang for his choice of camera angle, pace, and mood.[13] The reviewers in both *Time* and *Newsweek* claimed that *You Only Live Once* was the best crime movie since *Public Enemy*, William Wellman's famous 1931 movie with James Cagney. Both critics were struck by the film's social comment, and the reviewer in *Newsweek* wrote at length about the research into prisons Lang did before making the film.[14]

Beyond a Reasonable Doubt (1956)

Two of Lang's earlier films—*M* and *You Only Live Once*—dealt effectively with the theme of capital punishment, and in the midfifties he returned to the theme with less satisfying results. The case against capital punishment was clearly made in the earlier films: the killer in *M* was emotionally unable to control his urge for murder and needed a doctor more than an executioner; Eddie in *You Only Live Once* is sentenced to die for a crime of which he is innocent. But in *Beyond a Reasonable Doubt* Lang's attitude toward this social issue is not so clear; and as a result this film, the last one he was to make in America, remains far less successful than the earlier ones.

The opening scene shows promise of the earlier Lang as we are taken into a prison and shown the electrocution of a criminal. This is the sort of visual realism that created the mood of *You Only Live Once*. Even the debate between a writer and a newspaper editor over the merits of capital punishment is palatable; Lang had given mini–sermons in many of his films, including *M* and *You Only Live Once*. But when the two men begin to plan to frame the reporter in order that an innocent man be sentenced to death so that the writer will have the subject for his next book, the film begins to fall apart.

The men plot to have the writer, Tom Garrett, found guilty for the murder of a stage girl. They plant the evidence, but they also document their actions with photographs which include the front page of a newspaper to prove later that Tom created the evidence after the crime. The editor keeps the photographs with the intent of using them to save Tom at the last minute after the innocent man has been condemned to death on circumstantial evidence. After a lengthy trial, Tom is indeed found guilty and sentenced to death. The editor leaves his home to get Tom freed but is killed in an automobile accident before reaching the authorities. The editor's daughter, Susan, who is, of course, in love with Tom, believes his story and, as her father's replacement, puts the resources of the paper behind the effort to prove him innocent. The effort seems doomed to failure until at the last moment, the executor of the editor's estate runs in to say that he had found in the papers of the editor the evidence proving Tom innocent. Susan rushes to Tom to tell him that he is being released; but bitter and overly proud of his own intelligence, he reveals to her that he really was the killer. The entire story was his attempt to cover up the actual murder by drawing attention to facts that he could disprove (another use of misdirection). This plot device fails because we are so little prepared to accept the fact that the man we had rooted for for so much of the film should be exposed as the villain in the last two minutes of it. For a moment it seems that he will get away with the crime, but Susan goes to the governor and tells the truth. Tom is taken back to his cell. We assume that he was finally executed for murder, but Lang leaves this point dangling.

While the reviewer in *Newsweek* liked the film and claimed that people who enjoy unraveling mysteries would enjoy the film, most other contemporary reviewers saw the plot as improbable and of little cinematic value.[15]

The struggles in the film have been confusing. We watch Tom struggle against the death penalty, only to discover that his reasons are personal. Then we see him degenerate as he comes to believe that he will be executed when the photographs are burned. So far his degeneration is typical of Lang's work. But at the end we discover that this man does not seem to become degenerate because of what society does to him; he has been degenerate all along.

The experience with *Beyond a Reasonable Doubt* was not a pleasant one for Lang. He and the producer, Bert E. Friedlob, fought often over the content of the film. Lang wanted to open the film with footage of an execution similar to the documentary beginnings that had worked so well in *Clash by Night* and *Human Desire*. When he described to Friedlob what he had in mind, he was told to go ahead and make the scene realistic. But later when the producer heard what was being shot on the set, he stormed in and accused Lang of creating an excessively cruel scene. Lang felt betrayed, but this was not to be the last time. After constant fighting over the entire film and Friedlob insisting that the "cruel" shots be taken out, Lang became so disgusted he left the editing of the film to his cutter and walked out. The producer tried to entice him to come back, but Lang had had enough. He decided not to make any more films in the United States.

Social Commentator

There can be no question that Fritz Lang was a director with a social awareness. Even his films that were not on a social theme, such as *Western Union* or *The Big Heat*, contained elements of social commentary; the films discussed in this chapter have obvious social themes. Lang seems to have struggled to combine his social attitudes with the commercial considerations of making a film. He wants to make a point but he also worked in a system that insisted on profits. Few other filmmakers have so successfully combined the message film with economic viability.

But there is a hitch in a treatment of Lang's social films. The final effect of these films is not social outrage, as in the Third World films; I do not remember *Fury* as in indictment against lynching or *M* as a message to mothers about their care of their daughters. I remember the face of a man about to be burned alive or of a woman so distorted with hatred that she will set fire to that man. I remember the face of a man pleading with the members of his kangaroo court for understanding. I remember the love of a young couple trying to escape the law. I remember the look of a man who suddenly realizes that all his tricks have not worked and that he is about to be electrocuted. Somehow Fritz Lang has taken social situations and made us remember the people, not the situations. He has done this through the emphasis on the individual struggles of the people involved. Society's struggles are in the films, but in the final analysis Lang has made most real the struggles of the men and women caught in the confines of society's struggles. Peter Bogdanovich asked Lang during their interview whether *Fury, You Only Live Once,* and *You and Me* are not more concerned with the struggle of man against his destiny than with social protest. Lang agreed with this assessment and added ". . . the *fight* is important, not the result of it. . . . Sometimes, maybe, with a strong will, you can change fate, but there is no guarantee that you can. If you just sit still, however, and say, 'Well, I cannot do anything—' bang! At least you have to fight against it."[16]

Nevertheless, whatever Lang's highest priority may have been, many of his films exhibit his social conscience. The more important of his films of social protest are sincere, balanced, passionate, and successful as entertainment. They stand as disproof of one attitude that was common in the late thirties and early forties; Martin Quigley, editor of an important film periodical and influential at the Hays Office, wrote about another great film of social protest, *The Grapes of Wrath*: "The picture is a new and emphatic item of evidence in support of the frequently repeated assertion in these columns that the entertainment motion picture is no place for social, political and economic argument."[17] Lang, and Ford too, for that matter, showed that it was possible to combine good entertainment with a social message and to heighten both with good character development and analysis. *M* and *Fury* especially stand as evidence that entertainment and social protest can be joined into a single work of art.

Peter Lorre as the child-killer in *M*.

7

The Struggle in the West

FRITZ LANG'S THREE WESTERNS have not been taken particularly seriously by the critics and reviewers. In talking about *Man Hunt* Douglas Churchill wrote in the *New York Times* (May 11, 1941) that this about-to-be-released film was Lang's "first film of significance in over three years." The insignificant films Churchill was dismissing included both *The Return of Frank James* and *Western Union*, Lang's first two Westerns. Gavin Lambert in his excellent article, "Fritz Lang's America," does not do much more than barely mention the Westerns. And Allen Eyles, in his reference work on the Westerns, dismisses Lang's contributions to the genre as "not the most remarkable works of his long career," but Eyles does sense that Lang's artistic characteristics do come through.[1]

It is true that these Westerns are not as important in Lang's canon as some of the other groups of his films; for except for the use of color, Lang did not much stretch his imagination to discover—as he did in other films—technical innovations to express his theme. He primarily made these films for money; and although they embody the dark struggle, they are technically ordinary, with a few exciting exceptions. It seems to me, however, that these Westerns have been dismissed too quickly and deserve more attention for two reasons. First, they are an interesting study in what happens when a German intellectual filmmaker comes to America and begins to contribute to its popular culture. Lang had been so steeped in German myth it is at first strange to think of his working in a myth that is so obviously American as the Western. But he sensed the mythical nature of the American West and its importance to our culture, both popular and literary. He has said, "The Western is not only the history of this country, it is what the Saga of the Nibelungen is for the European."[2] His Western heroes are not unlike Siegfried in several ways: they are good men who are dragged down into vio-

117

Altar Keane riding her mount in Rancho Notorious
Credit: The Museum of Modern Art/Film Stills Archives

lence by forces even more powerful than themselves, and they are
strong men who ride out after a quest of some sort. In two of the
three Westerns, the quest for revenge plays just as important a role
as it did for Kriemhild. But Lang did not stop with simply recogniz-
ing the mythic qualities of the Western; he, this German expatriate,
helped to foster the myth of the American West. For example, the
first two of his Westerns project a type of hero only recently developed in films: the villain-hero. Both Frank James and Vance
Shaw are former criminals who are trying to go straight. They have
renounced their evil ways and are attempting to find a peaceful life
within the law, but society will not let them. Lang is obviously
taking a theme that worked well for him in *You Only Live Once* and
applying it to the west. He is therefore both borrowing from the
myth of the West and adding to it.

A second reason for reconsidering Lang's Westerns is that they
remain good entertainment. Recently I have shown both of the
earlier films to small groups of friends and they were both well
received. Whether these people would have paid money to see the
films in a theater is another matter, but the people enjoyed the
action, the color, and the usual treats from Lang's construction of his
shots.

The Return of Frank James (1940)

In an article in *Theatre Arts* Lewis Jacobs tells us that Lang was
given this completed script one day and told by the studio to begin
production the next: "He had to shoot cold."[3] Perhaps it is dangerous to analyze critically a film in which the director had so little
control over the plot, but Lang was able to leave his own stamp on
the film despite the short preparation period. At least it is possible
to give him credit for the strengths and blame the weaknesses on the
studio, without being contradicted.

In 1939 Henry King had directed a highly successful biography of
Jesse James, and Darryl Zanuck, thinking that a European director
might make a different type of Western, turned to Lang to make the
sequel.[4] Lang had lived among the Indians of the Southwest and
had written a script set in the West, so he was prepared mentally for
the assignment. He said that while he visited the Southwest he
looked at it through the eyes of a filmmaker.[5]

The sequel makes use of several of the actors from *Jesse James*,
playing their same roles. Henry Fonda, whose role as Frank in the

original had been secondary to Jesse's, was given the dominant role in this film. The sequel opens with the sequence of Jesse's murder shot from the original and then uses new material from that point on, much like Lang's continuation of *Siegfried* into *Kriemhild's Revenge*.

The first shot of Frank shows him plowing the field of his farm. The trees are in bloom and Lang, through the image of the coming of spring, gives the visual metaphor of Frank beginning a new life. When he receives the news of his brother's murder, his response is a sign of the reformed man: he will leave revenge to the courts.

When he hears that later, however, the jury found the Fords guilty of Jesse's murder but the governor pardoned them, Frank digs his neglected gun out of a feed bin and rides off to seek his own justice. He is a good man who is forced to do evil as a result of the actions of society, actions over which he had no control. Even though Lang did not write this script, it is remarkably well suited for him.

The Fords visit a local bar and invite others to have a drink on them, but the townspeople refuse. Here is the beginning of a shift in history in order to create myth. Early in the film the Fords have been called traitors for their betrayal of Jesse. Now they are depicted as the villains with whom no decent man would be seen. In real life there may, in fact, have been little to commend either of the Fords, but they did kill a wanted criminal. It is ironic that they should become the villains in our popular culture and their victim the hero.

Frank visits the crusty old editor of the town newspaper, Major Todd, to get the truth about the affair and to try to locate the Fords, who have just left town. To support his travels, he decides to rob the local railroad station—as part of the ongoing animosity to the railroad that began when the road was responsible for the death of the boy's mother. The robbery goes smoothly until it is interrupted by Clem, a young friend of Frank's who is determined to get an outlaw reputation for himself. Clem's gun goes off, accidentally alerting the town. The two escape through the roof and set out on a search for the Fords. They have become both the hunted and the hunters. During the chase the two meet a newspaper woman and give her a fictional story of the death of Frank in Mexico in order to mislead the authorities and the Fords. The connection with the woman, Eleanor Stone, begins a love element that rarely intrudes on the action of this plot, in the tradition of the good, old-fashioned Westerns of the thirties.

Clem and Frank find the Fords acting in a melodrama of the death of Jesse. Charlie and Bob ham up the show designed to make them heroes and Jesse the villain. Suddenly in the midst of the performance, Frank stands up where he had been seated. Bob sees him, panics, throws a lantern starting a fire and confusion, and runs. Frank follows them on horseback through the neighboring countryside, and finally Charlie's horse trips and Frank's falls over it. Both men are unhorsed and the expected gunfight results, but before Frank can shoot Charlie, Charlie slips and falls to his death over a cliff. This action perpetuates the myth of the good man trying to go straight. Frank has been responsible for Charlie's death, but actually he did not kill him. He had not killed the railroad agent shot in the robbery earlier although he has been accused of the crime, and now he avoids another murder. The Hays Office decreed that no killer could be a hero, so Lang—or the studio writers—was forced to find ways around this censorship. In this film he creates a gunfighter who never kills even though he gets his revenge.

This image of the good man is furthered by Frank's sense of humor and fair play. In the next sequence Clem and Frank are surprised in their hotel room by a railroad detective who has been tracking them. Rather than killing him, they jump him and leave him tied up hanging from a hook on the back of the closet door.

Eleanor tells Frank that the black man who had been left to tend the farm in Frank's absence had been arrested and is going to be hanged for taking part in the station robbery. The girl is outraged at the injustice and gets Frank to promise to help the man as soon as he has caught Bob. He rides off, but then decides he must go to the hanging in Liberty before it is too late. In a montage sequence Lang shows Clem and Frank riding hard to cover quickly the beautiful countryside. Finally they arrive at the railroad station and hold up the train in the most memorable scene in the film in order to ride by rail to their destination. Lang says they worked on the scene early in the morning to get the right light for Technicolor and to use the rented train before it had to start its daily run; they only had time for a single take. Lang must have been pleased with the review of the film by Robert Dana, which praises this scene for the effective use of color as the dawn comes up over the train.[6]

When Frank returns to Liberty, he is arrested and brought to trial. There he is defended by the major, marvelously overacted by Henry Hull, who makes fools of the sheriff and prosecuting lawyer, much to the delight of the audience. Just as the jury returns a not-guilty verdict, Bob Ford appears and Frank chases him out of the court building. Shots are heard and Frank arrives just in time to find Clem, who tried to stop Bob, dying in the dirt. After the boy dies, Frank races after Bob, who has fled into the livery stable. There is a good sequence here as Frank stalks the man through the interior of the stable. Bob gets off a shot or two but misses. Just as Frank is about to shoot, Bob falls dead from wounds inflicted by Clem. Frank has his revenge without ever killing a man.

Back at the newspaper office, the major dictates an editorial letter to the governor asking for a pardon of Frank, while Frank and Eleanor say their farewells as she has to return home. Frank says that someday maybe he will get to Denver to say hello.

This film is not a typical Lang tragedy. Frank is pardoned at the end and never suffers for his actions as a criminal. He remains calm throughout the movie and never degenerates physically, mentally, or psychologically. Yet the film does show Frank in a struggle against his fate, in the vein of the films from Lang's German period. First, Frank tries to plant a farm, but fate in the form of the railroad forces him to rob, to seek revenge, and to run when the robbery is fouled by another man. But then fate intervenes to help him when the revenge is accomplished without murder on Frank's part. The polar positions in this struggle between Frank and his fate are represented by Eleanor and Clem. Clem is the voice of violence and revenge; Eleanor is the voice of restraint. The climactic scene comes on the trail as the two men chase Bob. Frank has been thinking about Eleanor's plea that he rescue Pinky and tells Clem that he is going back. Clem becomes nasty and insults Frank, telling him that his first obligation is to revenge. Frank slaps the boy and in doing so commits himself to rescue rather than revenge.

The contemporary reviews of the film were mixed. Thedore Strauss, writing a review in the *New York Times* (August 10, 1940), said that drama was missing, possibly because Lang was forced to follow the dictates of the Hays Office about the goodness of the hero. The results were that Frank had to be depicted as both "dangerous and respectable," an impossible task. Robert Dana, on the other hand, was impressed with the entire production: "We can recall no previous Western that has combined so expertly the beauty of nature with the actions and laughter of men."[7] Both reviewers commented on the beauty of the West as depicted in Technicolor, a treat possibly no longer available for viewers. All the prints I located were in black and white because the color of the original stock has deteriorated.

Western Union (1941)

Better received by the contemporary critics was *Western Union*, the next film Lang was to make. Bosley Crowther wrote in the *New York Times* (February 7, 1941), "*Western Union* is spectacular entertainment—a 'Western,' you might say, with proper cinematic unity."

The credits for the film say that it is based on a novel by Zane Grey, but a controversy remains about the source that is interesting, but more important to Grey scholars than to those interested in Lang. Briefly stated, Fenin and Everson, in their respectable study of Western films, claim that the story came from a screenplay written by a man under contract to Twentieth Century–Fox and that the novel did not exist. When the movie proved popular, Grey's publishers had the novel ghost-written and issued under the name of Zane Grey, who had died two years earlier.[8] This contention is denied by another critic who says that Grey was signing copies of the novel before he died.[9] Carlton Jackson, in his critical study of the works of Zane Grey, never doubts that Grey was the author.[10] Lang himself says that the film was "made from a book by Zane Grey, but nothing from it was used in the picture except the title."[11]

Lang may have overstated the extent to which he did not borrow from his source, but not by much. There are significant differences between the novel and the film. It seems unlikely that an in-house writer at the publisher would have departed so radically from the plot of a film that had proven to be popular. It is more likely that a filmmaker for many reasons would change the plot to suit his shooting needs and the requirements of the Hays Office.

As the movie opens, Vance Shaw rides so hard to escape from a band of men chasing him that his horse becomes lame and has to be let go. Shaw on foot comes across a man and begins to steal his horse, but stops when he realizes the man is hurt. He helps the man and takes him to a nearby stage station for futher assistance and leaves. We discover that the man is Edward Creighton, the head of the group that is installing the lines for Western Union.

Later in town the company is hiring, and Creighton is building his staff. He is introduced to a man just hired as a hunter, who turns out to be Shaw. Creighton suspects there is a reason Shaw was running but says nothing. Creighton's sister Sue is present and becomes the love element in the film. Also joining the company here is Richard Blake, a tenderfoot from the East. Blake and Shaw, opposites in almost every way, do agree on the charms of Sue and become rivals for her attention.

Once the construction of the line begins, the men move out on the trail. One of Lang's best transition sequences is the one that takes the men from the town onto the trail. He was careful to authenticate the details of the work for Western Union,[12] and the rhythm of the work and movement and the excitement of men in action give a new tempo to the action.

Later one of the men is killed by Indians, and Shaw rides out to locate them. He finds the raiders making camp and gets the drop on them. Only then does he discover that they are white men who are disguised as Indians. They and Shaw are old friends; apparently this is the gang with which Shaw rode before he decided to make an honest living. Jack Slade tells Shaw that they are Confederate guerrillas working against Western Union because the telegraph will help the Northern cause. Shaw leaves them, but Slade is sure that Shaw will not tell the truth about the men.

Not much later the men working at the head of the line are attacked by Indians who are drunk and simply want more whiskey. Shaw tries to pacify them, but fights one who wants to steal a survey instrument. During the fight Blake shoots the Indian unnecessarily. Suddenly there is the message that the main camp is under attack and the party rushes back to help defend it. The attackers get away with the company horses, but scrutiny of one of their dead left behind reveals a white man in disguise. Later Creighton is forced to go to town and buy his horses back from Slade because he cannot prove Slade had nothing to do with the raid.

The army rides up and an officer says that the Indians have forbidden the company to take their lines farther into Indian territory because of the killing by Blake. At this, Creighton, Blake, and Shaw ride out to convince the Indians to change their minds. Through the use of water and the electricity of the line, the white men are able to convince the Indians that there is magic in the wire and not to interfere.

Back in camp, a man rides in to tell Shaw that Slade wants to see him. Once out of camp Shaw is captured by the gang and tied up. Slade says that they are going to burn out the company and they do not want Shaw in the way. As they ride off Shaw burns the ropes off his arms, but he arrives too late to stop the fire. The fire is one of Lang's best uses of Technicolor as the flames break through the darkness.

Shaw has his hands burned trying to rescue the others, but when the fire is over, Creighton demands an explanation from Shaw, who remains tightlipped but angry. Fired, he mounts his horse, but takes time to tell Blake that Slade is Shaw's brother and that he is going to town to stop the gang from harrassing the company.

The scene cuts to the barber shop in town where Slade is getting a shave and the rest of the gang is gathered. Shaw rides up and confronts his brother, who shoots him through the barber sheet. Wounded, Shaw fights back and kills three of the gang, but dies before he kills Slade. At this point Blake arrives and takes up the fight with Slade. He runs out of ammunition, but just then Slade dies from his wounds.

In the final scene the members of the company celebrate the completion of the line. Sue regrets that Shaw is not present but Creighton assures her that Shaw did his part.

This movie, like *The Return of Frank James,* does contortions to meet the code of the Hays Office. Shaw obviously had a criminal past, he allows the gang to prey on the company without confessing his knowledge of them, and he kills three men at the end; obviously he cannot be the hero of the movie and he cannot live. So he dies and gets what he deserves—at least according to the censorship board. The fact is that Lang managed to make him the hero, in part by giving him some of the best scenes and in part through the acting of Randolph Scott, who probably did the best acting of his career in this role.

The most important struggle is the one that takes place inside Shaw. He is torn between his past and his new-found loyalties to the company and its people. In a sense society has fated him in the same way that Frank James was fated. No matter how they try, they are forced to resort to violence.

The larger struggle—the men against the elements that tried to stop them from constructing the line—had to be created and invented. These are the elements that help to create the myth of the

West: man against nature, white against Indian, the company against range fire. But in history these events were not part of the building of the line. In reality the company had little trouble putting up the line; the only problem was the buffalo coming to rub the ticks out of their hides against the posts and knocking the posts over. Zane Grey, Fritz Lang, and Robert Carson, who wrote the script, had to invent the incidents in order to give the story conflict and create the sort of struggle Lang wanted in his films.[13]

Rancho Notorious (1952)

A decade went by before Lang made another Western. This film was created to be a vehicle for Marlene Dietrich, a fellow expatriate from Germany with whom Lang wanted to make a film. He says that the experience was not what he hoped it would be. She was not anxious to play the role of a woman who was even a little past her prime, and she continued to compare Lang with Sternberg, who had made so many wonderful pictures with her. The results were mixed. She does not come across well for much of the film, but there are moments during which she has magic. During one sequence in a dance hall the girls ride their men in a charade of a horse race. Dietrich forces her "mount" onward in a manner reminiscent of her treatment of Professor Unrath many years before. And in other places in the film Lang took advantage of her beauty and photographed her in such a way as to make her beauty stand in stark, visual contrast to the ugliness of the violence and the country that surrounded her. But somehow the movie does not seem to be about her at all; she becomes fancy window dressing for the main plot.

Rancho Notorious was the first Western to make use of a theme song. The "Legend of Chuck-A-Luck" opens the film and then is used as a linking device between the various episodes of the film. Despite the fact that Lang was fond of the song,[14] it is, to me, harsh music by today's standards. The song, however, does set the theme for the film, and in fact also can be used as the theme song for many of Lang's films that deal with the dark struggle:

. . . Listen to the legend of Chuck-A-Luck, Chuck-A-Luck—
Listen to the wheel of Fate;
As round and round with a whisperin' sound it spins,
It spins the old, old story of Hate, Murder, and Revenge. . . .

"Hate, murder, and revenge" constitute the struggle for *Rancho Notorious* no less than in the Nibelungen films and others by Lang. The opening sequences establish the love between Vern Haskell and his girl and then show her wanton murder by two men. Vern tracks the two men and catches up with one of them just as he is about to die from a gunshot wound inflicted by the other. Vern learns from this man, by withholding water from him until he talks, the one word "Chuck-A-Luck," a term for vertical roulette. Vern, anxious to find the other man who should bear facial scars from his encounter with the girl, sets off to discover the reason the dying man used the word. He is motivated by his hatred and his need for revenge, emotions that change an innocent man into one capable of almost any act that will help him quench his thirst for violence. Like many of Lang's heroes he degenerates as the film progresses, both morally and physically. Visually we see him turn into a snarling, disheveled man dressed in dark colors. Still he stands out visually from Altar Keane (the Dietrich character) and her boyfriend Frenchy Fairmont, whom Lang dresses in black. By the end of the film Vern's revenge is complete, but he is now committed to a way of life outside the law. At one point in the film Altar tells Frenchy that she does not want Vern to become involved with the gang because he is not an outlaw. At that time he was not, but the sort of degeneracy Vern accepts cannot be reversed. Once he commits himself to violence, there is no means of rediscovering the innocent man of the opening sequence. In the final sequence he rides off with Frenchy; the ballad tells us that they were to die fighting.

The narrative technique of the film is more like the techniques Lang used in his German films than it is like the rest of the American ones. The frame is not too surprising in that Lang builds the plot around Vern's search for the killer. This part of the narrative is a conventional quest: first he has to identify Chuck-A-Luck, then find the ranch by that name, owned by Altar, and finally make himself welcome there among the criminals who use the ranch as their hideout. Once he is a member of the gang, he spends his time trying to identify the gang member who has killed the girl. At the end as he does so, he finds that his revenge has exposed both Altar and Frenchy to a threat from the gang, which believes itself betrayed. He is then forced to defend the two; in the battle Altar is killed but Frenchy and Vern drive off the rest of the gang.

What is unusual about this narrative technique is the extensive use of flashbacks to provide the background for Vern's quest. As he searches for Chuck-A-Luck and Altar, Vern questions the people he meets about the woman. Their accounts of her past and their remembrances of her contribute some of the film's finest moments and give Dietrich some of her best scenes.

Today's critics rate *Rancho Notorious* as the best of Lang's Westerns,[15] but in its day the critics did not give it favorable reviews. Bosley Crowther in the *Times* was disappointed at the Dietrich role because Lang did not give her much to do of consequence. He called the film run-of-the-mill despite the rather good fight scenes.[16] Alton Cook, writing for another New York newspaper, said that it had everything one might want in a Western—"except entertainment value." He concluded, "Along with all its stars, the film has Fritz Lang, no less, as director. It's like sending for a piledriver to crush an ant."[17]

The World of Lang's Westerns

Other directors of Westerns have been impressed by the struggles between the whites and the Indians or between man and nature; these elements naturally exist in Lang's Westerns. But the emphasis, as in so many of Lang's other films, is on the struggles within the individuals. Frank James is trying to lead an honest life, but the call to revenge is too strong for him. Vance Shaw likewise wants to forget his past, but the gang persists in reminding him of what he had been and puts in jeopardy his new life. Vern Haskell is a decent man who is destroyed by his desire for revenge. These are personal struggles. Frank survives his; the other two win victories of sorts, but are ruined in the action. Vance is ennobled by his defeat, as is Frank by his victory; Vern's corruption is too deep for redemption.

This is a world of violence and beauty in contrast. Altar Keane becomes a metaphor for this aspect of the West. Aging, she is still a lovely woman, and several of Lang's shots capture beautifully that aspect of her. But in them she is dressed in black, a reminder of the violent world she supervises as the mistress of Chuck-A-Luck. The films, all in color, are full of beautiful natural scenes into which humans introduce violence and evil.

8

The International Struggle: War and Espionage

INTERNATIONAL POLITICS have given to Lang an almost ideal background for his stories of struggles because conflicts between nations on a large scale also involve conflicts among people and within individuals. Lang made a number of films dealing with international struggle; but true to his theme, he always kept the individual struggles in the foreground and placed the larger struggle between nations in the background. His emphasis is on the character of the people involved in the international struggle rather than on the fates of the nations pitted against each other. But his political beliefs are never far under the surface. So these films are obviously political, but the ideology is presented through people who suffer and get hurt rather than through impersonal armies or bureaucracies.

Lang never hesitated to use his films to make a personal statement about politics, and his own experiences with the Nazis clearly affected his artistic work. Even the films he made primarily for commercial reasons under the influence of the Hollywood system are fraught with clear-cut political ideology.

Despite the obvious political comments made by the films and the Langian struggle between the forces of the decent government against the forces of the government that wishes to oppress, the emphasis of the films is on the individual men and women who are part of that larger struggle. Lang perhaps presented his ideology in allegorical terms in early films, such as the Nibelungen Saga and *Metropolis;* but by the time he made most of his political films, he had come to understand that the theme of the struggle is best depicted through the actions of people who are clearly individualized. Lang always tended toward the use of stereotypes, but at least in these later films his major characters are more than mere representatives of the larger forces. They are themselves involved in their

129

Guerrillas, Coke, and the American Flag greet the returning American troops in The American Guerrilla in the Philippines
Credit: *The Museum of Modern Art/Film Stills Archives*

personal struggles. The outcome of their struggles may well destroy them; it will certainly change them. Unfortunately, Lang usually also allowed his major characters to be spokesmen for his own political ideology, a trait that becomes a weakness in the films in which the flow of images and actions is broken by excessive political dialogue, as in *Hangmen Also Die!*

This combination of commerical appeal and political ideology is balanced well in a film such as *The Last Will of Dr. Mabuse*, already discussed in Chapter 5. In this film the criminals spew Nazi slogans, and Lang must have enjoyed the sight and sounds of his master criminal parodying the leaders of the party that was just coming to power. In this film, however, while the politics are recognizable, they are not so intrusive as to become obnoxious. The film is basically a crime story in which politics become one justification among several for the actions of the criminals. The political comments are clear but not intrusive; they are present without being dominant. In this film the struggle is between the criminal forces and the police trying to save the order of society, but the political comments add to the struggle a tale of the attempts of evil people to gain power by subverting the needs of the individual members of the gang to the wishes of the state. It is not the ends desired by the criminals that are political; it is their method.

Spies (1928)

Following closely the patterns of the Dr. Mabuse films is *Spies*, Lang's 1928 silent thriller. The film opens with the theft of copies of a secret international treaty. A foreign agent, Donald Tremaine, is brought in to help the local forces find the thieves and protect the treaty. No sooner has he arrived than the criminals behind the thieves discover his identity, and a lovely woman spy, Sonia, is sent by the gang's leader, Haghi, to find out more about the treaty from Donald. Rather than fighting and manipulating each other as good spies should, the two begin to fall in love. When Sonia returns to Haghi to ask to be taken off the case, he recovers her loyalty by reminding her what the government has done against her family.

The two lovers meet that evening for dinner, but when Haghi appears and reminds Sonia of her duty, she leaves. Her desertion of Donald causes him extreme anguish which leads him to a bar where he tries to lose his sorrow in drink. Suddenly a strange Oriental man, Dr. Matsumoto, appears and comforts him. This man is an agent of the Japanese government present to represent his government in the treaty transactions. He gets the drunken Donald into a cab and heads home himself in a heavy rain. On the street he comes across a young woman, nearly drowned in the rain and frozen in the cold. In reality she is Kitty, another of Haghi's women spies. Matsumoto takes her home and warms her, and she begs to stay. We are reminded of his sense of duty in a scene in which he sends three Oriental men off with three different packets, supposedly containing the treaty. Naturally all three are captured and their packets taken to Haghi, who discovers that they contain only newspaper. Back at the apartment Kitty seduces Matsumoto and, while he is asleep, steals his copy of the treaty. When he awakens and realizes that his own carelessness has led to failure and the needless sacrifice of three men, he gracefully follows the rituals of hara-kiri.

As the scene shifts, Donald prepares to attempt to smuggle the final copy of the treaty out of the country with the help of another agent, a clown who has made arrangements for Donald to take the train out of the country. At the same time, Haghi, who has been holding Sonia captive, asks her to run one errand for him and promises to release her to go to Donald when the chore is finished. She too goes to the train station and sees Donald on his train as it pulls out. When she hears that his train has crashed, she gets off hers and rushes to the crash site, getting to Donald just seconds before Haghi's agent does. In a strange fight amidst the wreckage, the two lovers defeat the crook and a chase begins. The police break into the bank owned by Haghi, but are unable to discover his hideout in the secret passages of the building, where he is again holding Sonia hostage. He gives the police fifteen minutes to clear out, or he promises to kill her. Donald leads the police on a frantic search while Haghi flees the building and Sonia manages to escape. When a grenade explosion reveals the secret rooms to Donald, he and his girl friend are reunited and all the crooks and spies but Haghi are captured. Donald and his boss realize that the only person who knew enough to have wrecked the train with Donald aboard was the clown agent. They rush to the theater to arrest him, now knowing the clown to be another disguise for Haghi. They arrive in the middle of his clown act, and he, sensing that he is about to be taken, uses a gun that is part of his act to kill himself. The audience in the theater thinks that this is part of his act and applauds as the curtain falls and the film ends.

Spies: The superimposition of the Japanese flag and messengers over the guilt-ridden Matsumoto

The film is up to Lang's usual quality of visuals. The opening sequence of the series of robberies and murder is told with great economy. A few well-chosen shots of hands opening a safe and of hands snatching a packet from an open touring car make clear the whole story of the crime. Lang uses a superimposition of the faces of the three slain messengers and the Japanese flag over the figure of Matsumoto to make visible to us the anguish he suffers for what he has done to them. The film tends more toward Expressionism than toward realism, as do most of Lang's early films. During the fight in the wreckage, Lang gives us a shot of Donald's hand sticking out of the rubbish, holding a gun on the gangster. Realistically this is almost an impossible action but the visual effect is superb.

The film does have its international struggles between the forces of various countries and the criminals who wish to dominate the country, but the chief struggles are the smaller ones that concern individuals. Sonia struggles with her belief that Donald and the governments he represents have wronged her family. Her love for Donald makes her struggle more complex. Donald's conflict is between his duty to his job and his love for Sonia. When he realizes that he has been used by the woman he loves, he sinks into a

Langian degeneracy that is characterized by drink and despair. This degeneracy is seen visually through Donald's appearance at the bar. He is disheveled, drunk, and unable to think like an agent. The services of Dr. Matsumoto help to restore him to action, although this rehabilitation is not fully depicted in the film.

Matsumoto's struggle is the most genuine of the lot. He is a kind and sympathetic man who is destroyed by his own good nature. He tells Donald that men in service as they are should be wary of women. But when Kitty offers herself to him, he is unable to resist. Finally he gives in and the pain on his face when he realizes he has been betrayed is equaled only by our pain as we watch him draw the knife through his stomach and give it the final turn upwards.

Like Dr. Mabuse, Haghi is an enigmatic figure. In one guise he is a master criminal, in another a respected banker, and in a third a clown, but in all three he is a ruthless man who demands and receives loyalty. Kracauer says that Haghi is a man without real purpose: "the master spy indulged in the spy business for the sole purpose, it seemed of spying. He was a formalized Mabuse devoted to meaningless activities."[1] Kracauer seems to have dismissed Haghi's claim that "nothing can stand in my way. I'll control the world"—certainly not a "meaningless activity." It would seem that Haghi's struggle was an external one for world domination, but more important to the film is the fact that Haghi is the cause of the struggles in the rest of the major characters. He is then a catalyst for struggle.

Man Hunt (1941)

The first anti-Nazi film Lang made in the United States was *Man Hunt*, made in 1941 and based on a 1939 novel by Geoffrey Household called *Rogue Male*. The novel was perfect for Lang in many ways. The central character is a man who is opposed to the Nazis and goes hunting after Hitler—apparently for the revenge of the murder of his girl friend, but little is made of this motive. The political nature of the Nazis fades into the background, and this man is simply hunted by anonymous people and has to run for his life. The chief external struggle is between this man and the one man who persists in the pursuit of him. The chief internal struggle is within the man himself. The events of the chase and of his internal struggles degrade him. Morally, he degenerates to the point at which he will commit murder, once with great deliberation and

forethought. Physically, he degenerates to living in a mud hut under
a briar patch. Despite this degeneration and his mental errors, the
man survives and perhaps even finds some purpose for himself in
life. Lang modified the story somewhat (actually he did not write the
screenplay) to make the Nazis' role in the struggle clearer and to add
a little propaganda. There is also the addition of a girl to add a little
spice.

The story opens with a man drawing a bead on Hitler through a
high-powered rifle. He pulls the trigger and there is only a click
from the gun; the chamber is empty. The man is about to leave, but
changes his mind, stops, and inserts a shell into the chamber and
begins to take aim again. Just as he is about to shoot, a guard
surprises him.

Inside the headquarters building a suave German officer, Quive-
Smith, interrogates the man, an Englishman named Thorndike. But
when Thorndike escapes, he sets out for England with Quive-Smith
close behind. As his ship lands, Thorndike realizes he is almost
surrounded by enemy agents and hides in the hallway of an apartment building. Here he surprises a girl on her way out and forces
her to help. The girl, Jerry, is a prostitute (the censorship code did
not allow Lang to make her occupation too clear)[2] and is not accustomed to genuine gentlemen but agrees to help him escape.

Before leaving, Thorndike wants to buy Jerry a present for help-
ing him and the two go to a pawnshop, where she picks out a rather
cheap-looking arrow pin. On their way out of town, they enter the
subway station but realize they have been spotted. Thorndike has to
kill one of the men in the subway tunnel, but the two escape. He
tells her where he will be in three weeks and on a lonely bridge they
tell each other good-bye.[3] When she returns to her apartment she
finds the Nazis waiting for her.

The scene shifts to a small village post office three weeks later.
When Thorndike checks his mail, he is followed by Quive-Smith to
his hiding place, an underground cave. Trapped in the cave,
Thorndike discovers that Quive-Smith wants him to write a letter
implicating his government in the assassination attempt. Of course
Thorndike refuses. Quive-Smith tries to make his captive see himself as a killer and gives him through a small hole in the wall Jerry's
cap with the arrow pin. Thorndike loses control when he understands that she has been killed to get at him. In this degenerate state
he finally admits that he had subconscious reasons for killing Hitler

and quickly he begins to plot the death of his captor. He fashions a makeshift bow and arrow, using the pin for an arrowhead. Slowly he takes aim through the hole in the wall at Quive-Smith and shoots. Quickly then he crawls out of the cave, only to be shot by the dying Nazi.

The next sequence is a series of war shots and then some of Thorndike in a hospital. Then he is released and joins the RAF. We see him board a plane for a trip over Germany and bail out. As he floats down in his parachute, a voice tells us that somewhere in Germany there is a man with a high-powered rifle and the ability to use it. Someday he will use it to get Hitler.

This story makes for a tight, suspenseful film that remains good entertainment. As propaganda its importance is slight, but the acting is solid and Lang's touches make some of the scenes memorable. The opening sequence of the sporting stalk of Hitler establishes the pace and suspense for the film. After long breathless moments the audience wants to yell out, "Shoot him, shoot him, damn it." But we are denied and the suspense continues. Later in the subway tunnel Lang uses the tunnel to frame Thorndike and the man chasing him in almost perfect geometric stylization. The parting scene on the bridge takes place on a set that uses street lights (actually only light bulbs made to look like street lights) to pull the eye of the viewer into the fog in the background, into which Thorndike is about to disappear. The fog becomes a metaphor for what is about to happen to the man. (See Chapter 2 for a detailed analysis of the struggles in this film.)

Hangmen Also Die! (1943)

Lang's next film about the Nazis was made in 1943. Bertolt Brecht had just fled to this country from the Nazis, and Lang asked him to collaborate on a screenplay. Lang worked closely with the recent immigrant because he believed that he knew the American audiences better, but Brecht's contribution of several important scenes makes his part in the filmmaking significant. Unfortunately the Screen Writers Guild saw the situation different and awarded the credit for the screenplay to John Wexley, who had been hired to put Brecht's words into English.

Brecht's primary experience was, of course, in writing for the stage rather than films. Despite the fact that both plays and films depict people interacting for an audience, there is a basic difference that results from the nature of the media. In a play the characters tell the audience what the author wants them to know. The fact that we in the audience see the actors speak their parts adds to the enjoyment of the experience but does not noticeably alter the amount of knowledge delivered about what is going on. In films the filmmaker allows the audience to see what is happening and the dialogue becomes auxiliary to the visuals. The result is that the good stageplay is more talkative than the good screenplay. This all leads us to one of the chief problems with this film. It is probably the most talkative of Lang's films. There are good scenes in which his characters discuss at considerable length their political views, but little happens visually on the screen. The scenes are good theater but only fair film. This effect is probably the result of the influence of Brecht on the film.

The plot was taken by the authors from the actual assassination of Reinhard Heydrich, Reichsprotektor of Czechoslovakia. The movie opens with the death of Heydrich, but we do not see the actual murder. Instead we see his assassin running from the scene, chased by the Nazi police but aided by a young woman. As the plot develops, the murderer, Dr. Svoboda, is befriended by the woman and her family, headed by a Czech patriot, Professor Novotny. The police arrest the professor and other men as hostages and insist that they will start killing them unless the murderer is turned in by the patriots. Mascha Novotny goes to the doctor at his hospital to beg him to surrender in order to save the rest of the men, including her father; but the doctor is convinced by others that his symbolic act of defiance will help ignite the country. Mascha goes to report Svoboda to the Nazis, but the scenes of totalitarianism at the police headquarters change her mind. The members of the underground decide that they must find a scapegoat for the murder. When one of their number, Emil Czaka, is shown to be a double agent, they decided to frame him. An elaborate scheme to make it seem that Czaka is the one the Nazis want is executed, and finally the Nazis accept him as an offering, freeing the Czech patriots. In the final scene a Nazi officer writes a report to Berlin saying that they know that Czaka was innocent but were unable to capture the real murderer. Czaka was a convenience to allow them to close the case.

Despite the lengthy dialogue, Lang managed to find numerous visual effects that demonstrate his control over his subject. The film opens with shots of Hradčany Castle, a beautiful Czech landmark.

These shots are accompanied by soft, lovely music. Then suddenly the camera cuts to an interior shot of a hall decorated with a large Nazi eagle and a portrait of Hitler. The music now is harsh. In this setting the Reichsprotektor enters and begins to humiliate the Czech citizens assembled for his benefit. The visual contrasts between the Nazis and the Czechs are emphasized through the metaphor suggested by the buildings and decoration. Later in the film the metaphor is repeated with different visuals. Again the Czechs are represented by the lovely buildings of Prague: the medieval spires and clocks suggest strength and warmth. This time the cut is to the funeral bier of Heydrich. The scene is cold and unemotional. The guards are erect but with no apparent concern for their duty. The scene has the typical Langian geometric stylization, and a certain stark beauty results, but when we compare this funeral with Siegfried's, we come to understand what difference the lack of emotion in the characters present makes to our reaction to the scene.

The political struggles in the film are clearly defined: the Nazis and evil vs. the Czechs and good. But again the personal struggles are more important to the appreciation of the film. Svoboda's conflict is between his humanitarian desire to save people by turning himself in and his knowledge that to do so would destroy the symbolic significance of what he has done. Mascha's conflict is between her love for her father and her sense of patriotism (and not, incidentally, her growing love for Svoboda). These struggles and those for the Czech citizens are, of course, made necessary by the existence in the country of the corrupting force of the Nazis, and that external struggle is never far in the background.

Ministry of Fear (1944)

The Graham Greene novel on which *Ministry of Fear* was based creates an ideal situation for Lang. The novel presents a man who, just released from a mental-hospital prison, is chased by unknown forces and led to believe that he really is insane after all. There is some question about the man's identity after he loses his memory as a result of a bomb explosion. Much of the novel is dreamlike and well suited to Lang's use of halluncinations. But the most obvious attraction of the novel to Lang is the fact that the enemy is the Nazis.

Lang changed the hero. In the novel he is easily sidetracked from his search for the truth and is not overly intelligent. In the movie Lang makes him more self-confident, more intelligent, and more determined.

As Jensen points out in a lengthy comparison between the novel and the film, the novel's presentation of the hero is more subjective than that of the film. Stephen in the novel is more likely to question his motives than is his cinematic counterpart.[4]

As the film opens, Stephen, just released from the hospital, wanders into a small church-sponsored bazaar where he is accidentally given a cake that was intended for someone else.

When his train finally leaves for London, Stephen's car is shared with a blind man to whom he offers a piece of the cake. During an air-raid blackout, the supposed blind man knocks Stephen down, grabs the cake, and jumps out of the train. Stephen follows in time to see the man blown up by a stray bomb. Going on to London, he decides to try to find the people responsible for the cake.

His trail leads him to the headquarters of the group that sponsored the bazaar, where he meets the brother and sister who run the organization.

The brother, Willie, befriends Stephen and takes him to the home of a fortune-teller whom Stephen may have seen at the bazaar. A quick glance at the woman tells Stephen she is not the one for whom he is searching, but she invites them to take part in a seance that is just beginning, and they stay. The plot here is complicated by the presence of the man from the bazaar for whom the cake had been intended, but his connection with the fortune-teller and the brother is not clear. The confusion here is well hidden by Lang in the visuals of the seance, which create a nice sequence with special lighting effects and some superimposition. When suddenly a shot rings out, the man from the bazaar falls dead, and Stephen is left holding the gun. This scene is a good example of Lang's use of misdirection. At this point we cannot be sure whether Stephen is a hero or a villain, whose side Willie is on, or who the rest of the people are. Above all, we cannot be sure whether Stephen is sane or insane.

After his escape from the seance, Stephen calls the sister, Carla, and asks for help. As they meet, an air-raid siren sounds and they rush to shelter. In this idyllic moment amidst a bombing Stephen reveals that he had been committed to the hospital for the mercy killing of his wife.

After the air raid the two set out to try to unravel this mystery. Agreeing to deliver a suitcase for a man who has befriended them, they narrowly escape death when the suitcase explodes. Stephen awakes in a hospital to find a Scotland Yard detective there looking for clues to the murders committed earlier. The detective does not believe Stephen's ravings about spies and Nazis and charges Stephen with murder. Stephen asks permission to return with the police to the site of the bomb explosion that killed the blind man from the train in order to find evidence that would prove his story. There, after a long search, they find the cake in a bird's nest (every now and then Lang creates scenes that are a little hard to accept). Inside the cake is a canister of film, which naturally turns out to be of military importance.

The trail leads the police and Stephen to a tailor shop. The tailor is the man at the bazaar who later was shot at the seance (speaking of misdirection!). He delivers a cryptic message over the phone about the delivery of a suit and then kills himself before the police can grab him.

Stephen rushes to the address where the suit had been delivered and, to the surprise of no one but Stephen, discovers Willie, who is the head of the Nazi spy ring. Carla joins in the fight against her traitorous brother, and when he runs from the room, shoots him through the door. Lang's best visuals in this film are the ones of the bullet holes appearing in the door and the light changing through them as the body falls unseen on the other side. The rest of the Nazis are about to close in on the frightened couple, but the police arrive just in time to rescue them. In the final scene Stephen and Carla are riding down the highway, making wedding plans.

Ministry of Fear is in one sense a good thriller, but it is too easy to figure out. Despite the fact that some of the plot devices tend to make it easy for us to anticipate the action, these same devices build suspense. For example, the tailor in the scene at the end dials a number on the phone with a gigantic pair of tailor's scissors, so large they are ludicrous. It stretches the imagination to believe that anyone would try to dial a telephone with so clumsy an instrument. So the action is fairly easily anticipated, but this ease of anticipation creates suspense. When is he going to strike and who will he strike? For many seconds we wait for something to happen. We know violence is at hand; we just don't know when or where.

Lang has managed to create in this film a good portrayal of

Lang and Gary Cooper study the script for *Cloak and Dagger*

paranoia. For most of the film Stephen cannot be sure whether he is being chased or whether his imagination only makes him think he is. Are there really Nazis all around him, or is he a sick man? Not only can Stephen not tell about himself, we in the audience are unable to tell. This film calls to mind Andrew Sarris's remark about Lang films in general: "Lang's films might be said to recall the century of Hitler and Hiroshima with the post-Freudian punch line: 'I'm not paranoid. I am being persecuted.' "[5] The real horror of the Nazis is that their insidious presence seems to corrupt before anyone realizes what is happening.

Parish and Pitts in their book on the great spy movies have given a fair appraisal of this film: "Although director Lang dismisses this effort ('I saw it recently on television, where it was cut to pieces, and I fell asleep'), it is essentially a good psychological thriller—atmospheric, and above all, engrossing to most viewers."[6]

Cloak and Dagger (1946)

Lang's last movie about the Nazis has its moments of genuine excitement and some of visual significance, but overall the film is uneven. *Cloak and Dagger* was made in 1946 in response to the considerable interest the OSS created at the end of the war when some of its activities were made public.

The film focuses on the recruitment of a scientist as an agent of the OSS and his activities behind the Nazi lines in Europe. Professor Jesper goes underground to find a woman scientist who has just escaped from Germany and is believed able to tell the Americans what progress the Nazis have made on the atomic bomb. Before she can help, she is whisked off by Nazi spies. The Americans raid a country farmhouse where she is held, but a German agent kills the scientist and ends the Americans' hope of easy information about the Nazi activity.

Jesper decides to contact an Italian scientist who had worked with the woman and who might be able to help. He goes into Italy at night by submarine and rubber boat and makes contact with an Italian agent of the OSS, a woman named Gina. The two plot to get Jesper in to see the Italian scientist; and once there, Jesper convinces the man to defect as long as he can take his daughter with him. Other agents go off to find the daughter while Jesper and Gina hole up in a small room. The love that develops between the two of them gives the espionage plot an interlude. Finally the word comes that the daughter has been found and that they must pick up the Italian scientist and take him to a landing strip for the trip out of Italy.

They arrive at a farmhouse near the air strip and await the arrival of the daughter. When she comes, it is quickly evident that she is not the daughter but a German agent and that their escape plans have been jeopardized. They are surrounded but try to fight their way out. Those who escape arrive at the air strip just in time to meet the plane. Gina refuses to leave because she has work to do in the underground. Jesper promises to return to her after the war and boards the plane. The last shot is of the plane in the air on its way home.

The struggle in this film is obviously between the good forces of democracy and the evil ones of the Nazis, but the problem here is that the war was over and the Nazis defeated. Why was Lang still concerned about their threat to mankind? Of course the Nazis (and the OSS) were still good commercial material for movies and Lang and Warner Brothers were strongly aware that such a film would sell well. But Lang's use of the Nazi seems different here. They seem to be a convenient metaphor for the abuse of atomic power, an abuse in 1946 far more likely of the Americans than of the Germans. Actually Lang made a different ending for the film that Warners cut out which reinforces this interpretation of the film. In Lang's original ending, the Italian scientist dies of a heart attack, leaving the Americans with only a photograph as a clue to the German productions of atomic power. The American agents are unable to destroy the Nazi atomic industry. Lang recalls that the final shot was of Jesper saying something like: "This is the Year One of the Atomic Age and God help us if we think we can keep this secret from the world, and keep it for ourselves."[7] It should be remembered that Lang returned to the theme of atomic abuse in *The Thousand Eyes of Dr. Mabuse*. He at least saw the struggle in *Cloak and Dagger* as something larger than a simple conflict between the Americans and the Nazis.

The interior struggles are important in this film also. Jesper is another of Lang's innocent heroes who is forced into a situation in which he performs acts that go against his character. Jesper would rather be finding a cure for cancer in his research laboratory, but instead he is out taking lives rather than saving them. Gina, too, feels the conflict. She is well trained in her profession and makes a good seductress in the line of duty. But her love for Jesper is sincere and shows her what she has sacrificed.

Parish and Pitts list the weaknesses of the film: the instruction of the love scenes into the flow of the spy story, the "forced humanitarianism" that Lang puts into Jesper's mouth, the acting of Gary Cooper as Jesper—he was just too American to pretend to be a German scientist.[8] Lang, on the other hand, had the greatest respect for Cooper, but found another weakness in the acting of Lilli Palmer as Gina. He said that she had no heart.[9]

As in many of Lang's films, the strengths lie in individual scenes that were photographed with a great understanding of the camera's ability to capture the mood. The opening sequence shows the murder of an agent in a small European café. It is shot almost entirely in black, with streaks of light highlighting objects, suggesting the action rather than explaining it. Another important visual scene is the fight between Jesper and a Nazi agent while Gina and Jesper are trying to pick up the scientist to go to the plane. This is a dirty fight, full of eye gouging and karate chops to the neck, that keeps the viewer on the edge of the seat. Lang was especially proud of this fight because of its realism. He had former OSS agents on the set to advise him and he believed that Cooper had been able to learn from their advice.[10]

An American Guerrilla in the Philippines (1950)

In 1950 Lang made his last film about World War II, but this time he shifted the scene to the Pacific. Made while America was embroiled in the Korean War, the movie is about America in her age of political innocence. The major theme seems to be about the role America has in saving the rest of the world from totalitarianism. Lang quite seriously allows this film to make a statement about the duty and right of America to be involved in the struggles of foreign nations. The final scenes of the film leave the viewer with a strong feeling of nationalism. As the Americans take over control of the Philippines and drive the Japanese out, the Filipinos help the Americans raise a United States flag over the island and cheer as the Americans parade down Filipino streets. The American guerrillas are given bottles of Coke (the ultimate mythical symbol for America) while the Filipinos wave small American flags at the victors. This naiveté captures well the spirit of America in the 1950s, at least as I remember it; this is, of course, the spirit that got us into Viet Nam and other painful encounters during the past two decades. *American Guerrilla* is part of the myth-making process that created that spirit.

The story line of the movie is not complicated. Ensign Chuck Palmer, an all-American boy, has been left on Leyte by MacArthur when the latter retreated in front of the Japanese advances. Palmer and a group of other Americans decide to try to sail out of the Philippines in order to join MacArthur in Australia and get back in the war. Their boat is wrecked by the first storm they encounter and Palmer swims the eight miles to shore, finds some sympathetic fishermen, and has his men rescued.

The Americans are hidden and protected by friendly natives, but they are disengaged from the war. They spend their time running rather than trying to fight. Finally they encounter a Japanese patrol and discover that battle gives them self-respect. Palmer is convinced to stay on Leyte and organize a radio system through which the American forces can be alerted to the Japanese movements. The Americans scrounge supplies and build a ragtag army out of the natives. The next several weeks are spent observing and avoiding the Japanese, but there is an interlude during which Palmer and the widow of a French planter meet at a dance and become friendly. To no one's surprise, except possibly Palmer's, Jeanne comes to him on Christmas Eve and they fall in love. Almost every one of Lang's war and espionage films has the action of the adventure broken by a love interlude such as this one. This is a rather nice but illusory way to fight war. Suddenly one of the men is bayoneted by the Japanese; and Palmer, as the ranking officer, is called upon to perform the surgery. He tries hard but fails, and the man dies. This death depresses Palmer, but Jeanne's support and and MacArthur's message, "I shall return," on a pack of cigarettes give him hope.

Later while radioing information, the Americans are located by the Japanese but manage to get back to the village base and Jeanne. There they are surrounded in a church, and Lang gives us one of his better battle scenes. In most of his war movies he so concentrates on the personal struggles that he does not photograph the battles between armies. Here the armies are no more than companies, but the battle is fierce (but not very bloody, in keeping with the conventions of the day). The situation for the Americans looks hopeless, but suddenly the big guns and planes of the returning American armies save this small group. It is at this point the Americans and Filipinos celebrate the liberation of the islands.

There is not much to commend this film. There are a few scenes that stand out: the flood of people retreating before the Japanese, the ants crawling on the foot of the hiding soldier (mentioned in Chapter 3), and the church battle. But all in all, the film is schmaltzy, preachy, and unrealistic. The struggles are predictable and without the intensity of the struggles in the other war films. Lang says that he made the film for the money;[11] it shows.

The World of Lang's Soldiers and Spies

The world Lang has created for his war and spy movies is dark, unpleasant, and violent. It is inhabited by men and women who are anxious to dominate and control others for their personal gain. The exact nature of that gain is rarely made clear; what is clear is that the evil characters in these films will enjoy their struggle for power.

These are dark films made long before anyone ever heard of *film noir*.[12] Action often takes place in almost total darkness, and frequently it is impossible to distinguish the good person from the bad one. The darkness of the films (and even a color film such as *American Guerrilla* has most of its best shots in the dark) becomes Lang's statement about the darkness of the human soul that makes war and spies necessary.

The conventional film about war or spies is full of bloody violence and large battles between soldiers. Lang is not unaware of the importance of this violence, but his war and spy films make more use of personal violence. The struggles he puts his characters through in these films are the struggles between individuals rather than between armies. Basically his soldier and spy heroes are decent people who through innocence or idealism have become involved in a situation that creates a conflict between their morality and their cause. Captain Thorndike is a big-game hunter who no longer wants to kill animals, much less people. Dr. Svoboda is a medical man who is forced by his opposition to Nazi totalitarianism to kill. Professor Jesper would rather be working in his cancer laboratory than spying, yet he finds himself in a bloody fight for his life and willing to do just about anything to his opponent in order to stay alive. Chuck Palmer is almost the perfect boy next door—too perfect for realism. He is kind, democratic, patriotic, tough when he has to be. But war makes this sensitive, decent boy into a fighter.

Much of the violence in these films is psychological or mental. Dr. Matsumoto suffers greatly because he realizes that his own weaknesses have nullified the sacrifices of the lives of his messengers. The cat-and-mouse games the Nazis play in *Hangmen Also Die!* are perhaps worse than the overt acts of violence. First you are in jail, then you are free to go, now you are arrested again. And the struggles of Stephen Neale to discover whether he is sane or insane are complicated by people who care less about this man's mental health than about their own perverted cause.

All of these films, except perhaps *Spies*, are preachy movies which Lang has used to present his own ideological stance. He is never unaware of the commercial aspects of his productions—at least as long as he is making films in America—yet he never misses a chance to use the films to make his message. Some of the best anti-Nazi films from the period resulted, but frequently the ideology intrudes upon the art.

As a group these films have one characteristic that is missing from most of Lang's films: a happy ending. In all of these films good wins out over evil. There is, of course, suffering on the part of the good side, but in all of them in the final scene the enemy power that has caused the struggles and the suffering is defeated. Lang's view of man as having to endure and go on with whatever life is left is manifested in most of his films, and the final victory is rarely clearcut. Most of Lang's heroes survive, but they are bereft of family, freedom, or self-respect. But in the war and spy movies (and possibly in the Mabuse films, but that is a debatable issue), the heroes win. This change in Lang's vision results from the political aspects of the films. Lang felt strongly the need to have the forces of totalitarianism lose. He simply could not allow the Nazis to dominate the world. Even *Man Hunt*, made early in the Second World War before the Allies were able to turn the battles against the Nazis, has a strongly hopeful ending. The voice of the narrator as we watch Thorndike parachute into Nazi territory tells us that some day, somewhere, the assassin will kill Hitler. In these films the individuals we have followed so closely suffer, but at least their causes have dominated.

9

The Criminal Struggle

IN GENERAL IT MAY BE SAID that Fritz Lang's movies combine intellectual stimulation with terror; they place people in situations in which they must struggle against forces that cause terror. No group of films is better suited to illustrate this theme than those about criminals.

Lang had been attracted to detective and criminal stories almost since the beginning of his career. All of the Mabuse films, *Spies*, *M*, and even some of the war films make use of elements that are often associated with the criminal thriller. Lang's largest group of movies about criminals, however, consists of films he made in America toward the end of his career. These films have not received the critical attention of the earlier films, although they are shown on late shows on television, often in badly distorted prints. This neglect is unfortunate because several of these films remain good entertainment.

The Woman in the Window (1944)

Professor Richard Wanley, a professor with a specialty in the psychology of murder, sees his family off for the summer holidays and goes to his club for drinks and dinner with his old friends, the district attorney and a doctor. Dinner over and his friends having gone, the professor reads for a few minutes and then leaves the club, slightly inebriated. He stops to look at the portrait of a young woman on display in a shop window when suddenly the image of the model appears in reflection over the portrait (not unlike similar shots in *M* and *You Only Live Once*). The girl, Alice Reed, invites the professor to her apartment to see some of the sketches for the portrait. Just as they settle in, the girl's jealous lover breaks in, and the professor kills him in self-defense with a pair of scissors. He begins to call the police, but stops and reconsiders. Why get in-

149

volved when they could dump the body in the countryside? Lang
carefully builds the suspense during the sequence in which Wanley
disposes of the body. His nervousness and his carelessness tell us
that he must be caught; the only question is how.

The next night Wanley and his two friends again dine at the club.
While suffering from a good case of guilt, the professor remains calm
and has control of himself. But then he is invited to go with the DA
to the scene of the crime (as a professional criminologist). There he
begins to make mistakes; he is beginning to lose his composure.
Later Alice, who has not known his name, sees his picture in the
newspaper and calls. She is now confident, but he is weakening.
Without warning, the bodyguard of the slain man appears at Alice's
apartment and demands a payoff. When she calls Wanley, he calmly
begins planning to kill the bodyguard. He gives sleeping powders to
the girl with instructions to administer them in an overdose to the
bodyguard. When the suspicious bodyguard leaves the apartment
without drinking his medicine, Alice calls Wanley to tell him of the
failure. He goes to his bathroom and takes some of the powders
himself. At the same time back in the street outside Alice's apartment, the bodyguard is killed by police who think he is a prowler.

Professor Wanley and the body of his victim in *Woman in the Window*.
Credit: The Museum of Modern Art/Film Stills Archive

When they discover some of the evidence of the murder on him, they think they have solved the killing. Like Eddie in *You Only Live Once*, the professor is committing a fatal act at the moment external forces are freeing him. Fate does not always work against Lang's characters; sometimes their own actions counteract external Fate. Such films as this one demonstrate that in this country Lang's view of Fate shifted. He became far more interested than he had been in Germany in the possibility that character becomes Fate.

Alice runs to call Wanley, but there is no answer. He is conscious enough to hear the phone but not strong enough to reach it. Suddenly Wanley is awakened by the footman at the club. The entire episode has been a dream. The hat-check is the man he thought he had killed; the doorman is the bodyguard. Relieved and happy Wanley leaves the club but stops to admire the portrait in the shop window. Suddenly a streetwalker approaches, but he runs off shouting, "No! no!"

This conclusion has been roundly criticized. Gavin Lambert says bluntly that it is "indefensible."[1] Lang defended himself: "I rejected a logical ending because it seemed to me a defeatest ending, a tragedy for nothing brought about by an implacable Fate—a negative ending to a problem that is not universal, a futile dreariness which an audience would reject."[2] Lotte Eisner believes that this attitude demonstrates that Lang had developed beyond the "man trapped by fate" formula of the German films;[3] but since I do not believe that Lang even in the early films (with the possible exception of *Destiny*) ever depicted his characters' struggles as being completely controlled by Fate I am not surprised at his attitude here. He may well have been right about his audience. I do not quarrel with the ending so much as I do with our preparation for it. In two other films which readily come to mind because they contain the revelation at the end that the action has been a "dream"—*The Cabinet of Dr. Caligari* and "An Occurrence at Owl Creek Bridge"—the audience on reflection can understand that there had been clues throughout the films that what they were watching was hallucination of some sort. As we think back over the two films, we realize that we overlooked the clues and have only ourselves to blame for being surprised at the revelation of the dream/hallucination. In *The Woman in the Window* the clues are not there. We get the feeling that we have been tricked; being misdirected is one thing, but being tricked is another.

Putting the ending aside, the film is a pretty good view of a man's struggle in a criminal trap. We can understand his middle-aged-male frustrations and fantasies, and we can sympathize with him as he begins to degenerate under the pressures, even though he does some incredibly stupid things.

In many ways the film is vintage Lang. The entire film is hallucination, the decor is carefully designed to reinforce the characterizations (especially Alice's apartment), mirrors and unusual lighting effects highlight the characters. And the camera work is creative. Eisner quotes at length a letter from Nunnally Johnson, the writer-producer, which describes one shot in particular. At the end Lang moved the camera in on Wanley as he expires from the sleeping powders. Suddenly a hand comes into the frame and awakens the man. The camera pulls back, revealing him in his club with the footman beside him. During this one shot Lang has both changed the professor's location from his quarters to the club and changed his suit back to the one he wore on the night of the murder. All this has been done without a cut. While the camera was in close on the dying man for only a few seconds, the stage hands exchanged the set behind him and another man crept under him and pulled off his snap-away suit, leaving him in the suit in which he had fallen asleep.[4]

Scarlet Street (1945)

The next year Lang made another movie with the same stars—Edward G. Robinson, Joan Bennett, and Dan Duryea. This one was about a middle-aged bank clerk who becomes caught up in the midst of a murder. It is based on a novel, La Chienne (The Bitch) by Georges de la Fouchardiere. An earlier adaptation by Jean Renoir gave Lang and screenwriter Dudley Nichols the idea, but they refused to look at the earlier film again for fear it would influence them. Lang realized that the clue to an acceptable transformation of the novel was to move the action from Montmarte to Greenwich Village.

The establishing shot of a Village street in the opening sequence creates the atmosphere: exotic, a little seedy, appealing. The camera goes inside a restaurant to a banquet given in honor of Christopher Cross, a cashier who is being given a gold watch for twenty-five years service. When the bank president hurries through the ceremony because a lady is waiting for him, Chris wonders what

Credit: The Museum of Modern Art/Film Stills Archive

Chris Cross and his new-found love in *Scarlet Street*

it would be like to have a young girl love one. As he leaves the restaurant, Chris interrupts a fight between a girl and her boyfriend/pimp, and paternally Chris lectures her on being out so late. Both misunderstand the other's profession: she thinks he is an artist and he thinks she is an actress.

At home Chris is domesticated. His shrewish wife dominates him, but he rebels in small ways. He lies to her about the time he came in the night before, and every Sunday he retreats to the bathroom, where he paints, delighting in both the solitude and the knowledge that his wife does not like what he does. It seems that the impression he left with Kitty that he was a painter is only a partial lie. He does paint, but not for money.

At Kitty's apartment her boyfriend, Johnny, talks her into writing Chris to try to get money from him. Chris meets her at an outdoor restaurant; he is like a boy again (he whistles with the birds—the scene may fit his character but cinematically it makes me groan). She suggests that he set up an apartment where he can paint without the bother of his wife and then asks for money. He tries to borrow and to steal it but fails at both attempts. Later at home his wife goes out to visit a neighbor to listen to a soap opera on the radio

(ironically entitled "The Happy Household Hour"). Chris takes advantage of her absence to steal one of her insurance bonds.

An apartment is rented and Chris shows up with some of his
paintings. Johnny is present but pretends to be a friend. After trying
like a schoolboy to get a kiss, Chris leaves. Kitty tries to analyze the
paintings but does not understand them (another note of irony: one
of them is full of erotic snakes but the sensual side of the painting is
missed by this sensuous woman). Johnny takes the paintings for an
appraisal and discovers they are worthless. An art critic offers to buy
two and later seeks out the artist because of the primitive power of
the paintings. Kitty claims that she did the work and signs the
canvases. Chris discovers what she is doing with his work but in his
state of infatuation does not mind. He is pleased that his work is
being recognized. Kitty, using Chris's work, has a successful show at
a gallery.

The former husband of Chris's wife arrives, and Chris uses him to
win his freedom from the old woman. He rushes to Kitty's apartment to tell her that he is going to be free to marry her, only to
interrupt Kitty and Johnny in bed together. Both Johnny and Chris
leave. Chris goes to a bar and drinks, hearing over and over Kitty
saying, "Jeepers, I love you Johnny." He returns to the apartment,
and without understanding entirely what is happening picks up an
ice pick and stabs her. As Chris slips out, Johnny returns drunk and
gets arrested for the crime. In the meantime Chris is fired for steal-
ing from the bank.

Chris lies at court to insure Johnny's conviction. Johnny is taken
to prison to be executed. In his lonely hotel room, Chris deteriorates. He goes crazy with the memory of the love scene; the voices of
the lovers haunt him. He tries to hang himself, but is cut down
before he can succeed. He becomes a bum, wandering the streets.
He passes a gallery and overhears a conversation about his work,
one piece of which has just sold for thousands. But he wanders on
with the voice of Kitty loving Johnny echoing in his mind.

Lang says that the Hays Office gave him no trouble about this film
even though it dealt with a prostitute and a successful murderer.[5]
The reason for the lack of censorship is that Chris does not get off
without punishment. Eisner points out that at the end Chris is still
haunted by jealousy rather than guilt, but whatever is causing his
torment it has ruined him.[6]

Lang's portrayal of human misery has developed throughout his career, and no film better illustrates the point than this one. *Scarlet Street* deals with a nobody who goes through a struggle that is not noble or grand or worthy of much note by anyone else. Chris Cross is not a hero like Siegfried or even a master criminal like Mabuse. He is not even mistreated by society as are Joe Wilson and Eddie Taylor. In a sense he is more typical, more average, than the central figures of Lang's other major films. Middle-aged, shy, frustrated, Chris is like many of us; his problems are those that are understandable to many of us. His crime and his degeneracy are the result of his trying for once in his life to be more than he had been.

Most of the film is classic Lang: the psychological study, the chiaroscuro, the theme of the good man overwhelmed by evil—but there is one characteristic of the film that is uncharacteristic of the filmmaker. The film has humor. Many of Lang's movies contain what were supposed to be touches of humor, but most fail in this regard. Lang simply did not have the feeling for comedy; *Liliom* is the only general exception, but that film was not well received in its own day. But in *Scarlet Street* there are a few scenes that demonstrate first-rate comedy. Chris's use of his wife's first husband in order to gain his own freedom demonstrates that with the right material Lang could direct comedy.

Clash by Night (1952)

When Lang turned his attention to a play by Clifford Odets, the resulting film became a sensitive version of the pessimistic vision of life so popular on the American stage during the fifties. Unfortunately the film is cliché riddled: "Home is where you come to when you run out of places" and shots of a raging sea every time Lang wants to show anger building up inside a character. But the overall effect is good, and despite the flaws the movie engages the audience.

In some of Lang's films, such as *You Only Live Once*, the social protest is the dominant theme, but in *Clash by Night* Lang's social consciousness is used simply to establish an atmosphere. Lang and his cameraman spent several days in Monterey shooting footage of an old sardine cannery, the docks, and the sea. This footage was then used as the establishing sequence, which has a strong documentary flavor and which suggests a social theme.

Actually *Clash by Night* is not a criminal film since the anticipated crime never occurs. The situation is similar to those in *The Woman in the Window* and *Scarlet Street* in that a middle-aged man resorts to violence over a woman who has lately come into his life. In *Clash by Night,* however, the man stops just short of murder.

Mae Doyle returns to her hometown after years on the road. She is tired, a little cynical, and ready for someone to take care of her. A middle-aged, simple fisherman, Jerry D'Amato, falls in love with her and she agrees to marry him. She obviously is not excited by Jerry but he offers stability; she gives him a child in return. The need for excitement that had taken her on her wanderings for so many years leads her to be attracted to Earl Pfeiffer, the handsome and cruel projectionist at the local movie house. Their affair is finally discovered by Jerry, who first tries to forgive Mae and to convince her to stay. Failing at that, Jerry loses control and rushes to the projection booth to confront Earl. He has come to talk but quickly their conversation becomes a brutal fight in which Jerry almost kills Earl before Mae comes in and tries to stop the fight. When he throws her away, Jerry hurts her; the fact that he has hurt the woman he loves brings him to his senses and he walks out.

When Earl and Mae get to her house, they discover that Jerry has been there ahead of them and taken the baby. The two discuss the fact that this may be their last chance of happiness together. Earl cruelly tries to insult her into going with him, but finally she decides in favor of her husband and child. She finds Jerry at his boat and asks for forgiveness. At first Jerry resists her, but finally he gives in: "Got to trust somebody; there ain't no other way." He gives her the baby.

This brief plot analysis sounds a lot like a soap opera, but the film is raised above that level by the acting, the struggles, and the camera work. Paul Douglas gave a fine depiction of a middle-aged man trying hard to adapt to family life. His Jerry is warm and generous but accustomed to having his own way both at home and at sea. As captain of his ship, he has developed attitudes that are of little use around the house. He is unable to deal with a woman who is restless and intelligent. He has a conservative sense of what a family should be, but he struggles hard to accomodate Mae. He could be considered Lang's prototype of the good man who degenerates under pressure. Decent, but not any brighter than he has to be, Jerry does not know how to respond to his wife's infidelity (in all fairness to Jerry, I am not sure how any man—bright or not—should respond to such an event). At first he tries to achieve a reconciliation, then resorts to violence. This good man almost kills a man who had been his best friend. Somehow—how is not entirely clear—he overcomes the instinct for lashing out at those who have hurt him; perhaps it is the love he has for his child.

Barbara Stanwyck as Mae portrays a woman who has her struggle too. Mae is in the throes of the archetypal small-town struggle between the security the town offers and the excitement of the road. She understands herself well and knows that she may well make life miserable for Jerry. She longs for a comfortable man and would do anything for him, but when she has one, the old passions for the exotic surface. At first she does not try to resolve the struggle: she has both men at the same time. But when Jerry discovers the affair, she is forced to make a decision and the struggle can no longer be ignored. Finally she contrasts Jerry's dullness and kindness with Earl's excitement and cruelty. The events have taught her much about herself; she resolves the conflict by deciding finally that she is willing to take her chance with Jerry.

Lang's use of the camera has as usual reinforced the struggles. Early in the film when Jerry proposes to Mae, she is standing on some steps high above the man. He has to look up to her; he is humble; she is in control of the situation. Later after the revelation of the infidelity, Jerry waits for her to return to the house so that he can try to restore their marriage. This time he is up high and she on the beach below him. The camera set-up suggests that he has moral superiority on his side.

The Blue Gardenia (1953)

The next year Lang returned to the detective format for another suspense thriller, *The Blue Gardenia*. After *Clash by Night* Lang had gone for about a year and half without making a film because he had been on the blacklist as a suspected Communist solely on the basis of his liberal inclinations and friends. Finally Harry Cohn gave him a chance to make *The Blue Gardenia*; gratefully Lang accepted the job even though the plot was weak and he was given only twenty-one days in which to shoot the film (compare that with the sixteen weeks he took to shoot *Kriemhild's Revenge*). The results are not outstanding and even Lang dismisses the film lightly.[7] Lotte Eisner takes pains to try to find something nice to say about the film, but despite many typical Langian touches such as mistaken identity, mirrors, and hallucinations the film is missing the urgency of most of Lang's other films.

In terms of the dark struggle, however, the film is significant. Like Jerry D'Amato, Norah Larkin is a good person who is caught in forces that overwhelm her. In *Clash by Night* Lang used the shots of the storm at sea as a metaphor for the storm raging inside Jerry. In *The Blue Gardenia* the image for the metaphor is a whirlpool. At the moment she commits the crime that is going to trap her, Lang superimposes over her the image of the whirlpool to show that she is being dragged down by a powerful force.

Norah, despondent over a letter from her boyfriend in Korea telling her he is going to marry a nurse, accepts a date with Harry Prebble, who fancies himself something of a lady's man. In his apartment when he makes a pass, she at first hallucinates that he is the former boyfriend. When she realizes the truth, she strikes out drunkenly with a fireplace poker, shattering a large mirror in the process. She passes out, leaving herself and us with the impression she has killed Harry (another instance of Lang's use of misdirection). The result is that we share in her struggle with the guilt as we have the same information she does and believe with her that she is guilty.

She finally works up the courage to confess to a newspaper reporter who has promised in the paper to help the killer. Casey Mayo has staked his journalistic career on finding the killer, but when he discovers the truth, he has a small struggle of his own. Legally he is bound to turn her over to the police, but his emotions help him sympathize with Norah. His struggle is resolved when a bartender calls the police with the information he overheard when Norah was talking with Casey. She is arrested; but as Casey is leaving town, he hears a piece of music over the speakers at the airport and realizes the secret to the mystery. Norah had told him that as she struck Harry and passed out, the song "The Blue Gardenia" was playing on Harry's record player. But when Casey visited the scene of the murder, there was a different record on the player. Someone else had been in the room after Norah. He goes to the police with the story and they trace the record to a store. They discover the girl clerk who had sold the record to Harry and had then become involved with him. When she was later jilted, she had gone to his place and finished what Norah had begun. We can then remember that Harry had had a telephone conversation with this woman earlier, but at the time it seemed of little importance. Here, unlike *The Woman in the Window*, we have been given the clues that help us understand the ending.

Norah has survived her struggle, and like Jerry, her survival is the result of something indefinable in her character. Her innate goodness created the guilt that made her seek out Casey to tell the truth. That truth eventually led to his unraveling the mystery.

The Big Heat (1953)

Dave Bannion is a good cop and a good father and husband. Lang takes pains to establish these characteristics early in *The Big Heat* because Bannion too is going to degenerate under pressure. Lang himself says that the theme is "hate, murder, and revenge,"[8] the theme of *Rancho Notorious* as announced in its theme song. Like Vern Haskell, in the Western released only nineteen months earlier, Bannion becomes obsessed with revenge for the death of the woman he loved; unlike Vern he somehow emerges from the pits of degeneracy without becoming part of it.

Bannion's humanity is established through contrast with the leader of the gangsters, Mike Lagana. Both are family men, but there is an important difference. Lang shows Bannion at home with his wife as they love and tease each other. Bannion reads the story of the three kittens to his small daughter. This is a close-knit family but not an idealized one. Husband and wife do argue when he comes home tired and depressed, but it is their closeness that gives meaning to Bannion's life and that keeps him out of the sewer that surrounds his professional life. Lagana also is fond of his family, at least the part of it he discusses. No mention is made of his wife but he dotes on his daughter. He is furious when Bannion comes to his home because to do so brings the reality of the criminal world into the home he keeps for his daughter. And Lagana glows when Debbie, the girl friend of one of Lagana's henchmen, asks after the daughter. Yet Lang never permits us to see him love the girl; the two are never together in the film. We are given a glimpse of a party the girl is having when Bannion comes to the house, but the lack of scenes between the girl and her father makes us suspect that he holds on to the decent image of his daughter because she represents a vision of life this criminal can never attain. The irony is that after he becomes angry at Bannion for despoiling his house, Lagana himself plots crime in the house. Lang seems to have had a special reverence for the family (note the large number of his films in which the discord is the result of conflict within what otherwise would have been a normal family—the Nibelungen Saga, *Fury,* and *Clash by Night,* for example). The family relations of the central characters in this film become a metaphor for their decency. Lagana's most despicable crime occurs when he counters his concern for his own home and orders that Bannion's home be invaded. The result is that Bannion's wife is killed and his daughter is threatened. It is also probably worth considering that the other villains in the film have family problems. The policeman who kills himself in the opening sequence has gotten in trouble with the mob because he has fallen in love with another woman and needs money to leave his wife. And Vince Stone, the chief henchman for Lagana, is keeping Debbie without benefit of clergy; it is his treatment of her that drives her to betray him.

It is the challenge to his family that creates Bannion's struggle. After his wife's death, Bannion accuses the chief of police of being Lagana's man and loses his badge as a result. One of the other policemen tells Bannion that he should seek help from a priest because he is "on a hate binge." The hate binge drives him from the comfortable bungalow he had shared with his wife and which holds too many memories to a cheap hotel, whose decor Debbie describes as "early nothing." This is a variation on Lang's usual technique for showing degeneracy. Normally he showed the change in the character visually through the change in dress, but here the change in Bannion is demonstrated visually through the change in his environment. He goes from a nice home to a sterile hotel room.

One characteristic of Lang's theme is consistent. As in most of his films when the central character degenerates, he or she becomes isolated from other people, with the possible exceptions of one or two close friends or lovers. In general Lang's degenerated heroes stand by themselves, like Joe Wilson looking out of the window of the burning jail. Bannion too seems to lose all his friends on the police force and is left only with Debbie, the former girl friend of a mobster who is now severely burned as a result of the coffee Vince threw in her face: not, it would seem, strong support.

When Bannion goes to the home of the widow of the dead policeman to try to force her to confess her involvement with Lagana, he actually threatens her life. He is stopped by the arrival of policemen, and he goes back to Debbie at the hotel. This becomes a pivotal scene. First, he brings food to her and forces her to eat. He shows genuine concern for her, and we realize that his humanity is going to dominate. Now he is not so much alone. Then he tells her about his confrontation with the widow and how close he came to killing her. Debbie expresses our fears: "You couldn't. If you could, there wouldn't be much difference between you and Vince Stone." Beautiful but dumb Debbie seems to have put her finger on the central idea behind Lang's use of the dark struggle. Those characters of his that survive and emerge from it without surrendering to it are those in whom there is enough decency to keep them out of the pits of the degeneracy. Those that fail to survive are the ones who become so much obsessed by their passion, whatever it may be, that they become no better than the forces that drove them to the degeneracy in the first place. Here then is the chief difference between Bannion and Vern Haskell. Bannion, no matter how angry and hurt, cannot reduce himself to behaving with the cruelty of Vince Stone. He cannot injure or torture another just to satisfy his passion for revenge; Vern in *Rancho Notorious* can. We get a clue to his character early in his chase when he withholds water from a dying man until the man tells what he knows about the other man who had raped and killed Vern's girl. We should not be surprised when Vern and Frenchy ride off together at the end and the theme song tells us that they died in a gunfight. Vern cannot survive.

In the next scene we learn that Bannion has more help than he and we thought. He gets a call to go to the apartment where his daughter is being kept. As he enters, he is attacked in the hallway; we see all this action from his point of view and therefore assume with him that Lagana's men have his daughter and are about to capture him, too. But suddenly he discovers that this man and others are friends of his brother-in-law and are there to protect the girl. Bannion is no longer alone in his struggle. After he tells the girl the story of the three kittens one more time and goes out into the street, he discovers that even his friends on the police force have not forgotten him. His lieutenant and another man have come to watch over the apartment. Here within a few minutes Lang has managed to tell us that Bannion is one of his characters who will survive his struggle. He has found the fortitude to control himself with the widow, he has found compassion for the gangster's girl friend, and he has friends again.

The ultimate test of his recovery comes in the final scene when he has his predestined shootout with Vince. Vince has returned to his apartment to be greeted by Debbie, with a pot of hot coffee in her hand. When she gets her much-deserved revenge, Vince shoots her just as Bannion breaks in. The two men fire at each other in the dark until Vince runs out of bullets. Bannion has him now at very close range, knowing that this is the man who loves to torture women and who has just shot one of the two women Bannion could care for. Kriemhild, Chris Cross, and Vern Haskell could have pulled the trigger. Bannion cannot.

Human Desire (1954)

The next year Lang followed *The Big Heat* with another film that used the talents of Gloria Grahame and Glenn Ford. *Human Desire* was based on a novel by Emile Zola entitled *La Bête Humaine*; it had been made into an earlier movie by Renoir, but as with *Scarlet Street* the French film had little influence on Lang.

The problems in production with actors and location and the railroads were huge; unfortunately the results hardly make the effort worthwhile. The film is not one of Lang's best, but the theme of the dark struggle contributes to the suspense, and in a rather raw manner the film is a fairly good thriller.

Jeff Warren returns from the Korean War to his job on the railroad only to become immersed in a struggle for his decency. He meets Carl Buckley, the assistant yard manager, and becomes involved in Carl's life, at first without knowing it, then with full knowledge of what is happening.

Carl loses his job and asks his wife, Vickie, to go to her former lover, John Owens, who has control over Carl's job. She is successful; Carl suspects the truth about her methods and plots to kill Owens. He gets Vickie to write a letter to Owens to suggest that he meet her on a train in her compartment. When Owens arrives, Carl kills him and then uses the incriminating letter to force Vickie to stay with him and bend to his will. Jeff, who has been deadheading on this trip, chances upon Vickie as she leaves the compartment. Later at the police inquest of the murder Jeff lies about having seen Vickie; as a result, Carl and Vickie invite him to join them for a drink. Carl gets drunk and the other two have to help him home. After putting Carl to bed, Vickie lies about the murder. She says that she found Owens already dead. Vickie and Jeff fall into each other's arms and their affair begins. In the days that follow, Vickie becomes more unhappy with Carl's control over her and begins to use Jeff's affection as a means to escape Carl.

In one of the best-designed scenes in the film—one that reminds us of the better Lang designs from other films—the lovers meet in a shack beside the railroad tracks. She suggests that if he is a man, he will use the lessons learned in Korea and kill Carl. He tells her that it is easy to kill in war, but not so easy elsewhere. The scene is shot almost entirely in the dark and therefore stands in sharp contrast with the opening sequence (a bright montage sequence of trains that is reminiscent of the opening documentary nature of *Clash by Night*) and the closing sequence, both of which show Jeff in both physical and moral brightness.

Later Jeff follows the drunk Carl from a bar into the the rail yard; he picks up a wrench to use as a weapon. Just then a train passes in front of them and we are left to speculate about Jeff's guilt, in somewhat the same manner as we are left to speculate about Eddie's guilt in *You Only Live Once*. When Jeff goes to Vickie to tell her that he was unable to kill the husband, she becomes frantic. She alternates between telling him he is not much of a man and saying that she loves him. Through it all he comes to understand that he has been used and walks out, but not before he gives her the letter he has taken off the drunken body.

The next day Vickie boards the train on Jeff's run. Suddenly Carl appears at her compartment and begs her to return. He offers her the letter if she will only stay, but she laughs at him and says she already has the letter. The camera comes in for an extreme close-up to show the reaction of this man. He grabs her and kills her with his hands. Then he sits down. Forward in the cab, in full daylight (a decision that Lotte Eisner says Lang carefully and consciously made[9]), Jeff happily blows the whistle, sensing without knowing his freedom.

The chief struggle is obviously Jeff's. He is again another of Lang's innocent people who get caught in traps that offer the potential for destruction. He has, as the film opens, the opportunity for happiness with the daughter of an old friend, but he is more attracted to the exotic passion of a married woman. He makes his own choices; as Eisner says, "Fate is character."[10] The image of the hero has changed considerably during Lang's career. Jeff is no Siegfried caught by the forces of the gods. He is the all-American boy, returning from the wars with an understandable sex urge. He makes the decisions for himself and only he can be responsible for the results. His innate decency pulls him out of the darkness of the railroad shack and into the light of the engine cab. Like Dave Bannion he survives his struggle.

While the City Sleeps (1956)

Eisner says in the first line of her analysis of *While the City Sleeps* that it would be shortsighted to consider this film as simply a thriller.[11] It is, of course, more than that. Lang himself saw connections between this film and *M* and believed that this film too contained important social criticism.[12] Toward the end of his career, Lang made a number of films with simple plots, that is, films in which the struggle was superficial or confined to a single character (as in *Human Desire*); but with *While the City Sleeps* he returned to the type of script that offered him the complexity that had become Lang's signature in his earlier films.

The film depicts a number of struggles, both interior and exterior. Only two of them relate to the "thriller" aspect of the film: the struggle within the sex murderer and the one between him and the police as they try to find him before he strikes again. The killer is a boy/man who, driven apparently by psychological problems created by his mother, cruelly kills young women. The opening sequence demonstrates his method. As a delivery boy he gains entrance into this target's apartment, fixes the lock in passing so that he can easily regain his entrance, and then slips back to satisfy his urges. But he understands that he is driven by forces he cannot control, much like Franz Becker in *M*. After the murder he scribbles "Ask Mother" on the wall in lipstick. He obviously wants to be caught before he kills again. The camera follows him to his room where he watches the television newscast for the story of his murders. When the paper runs a front-page story with a sketch of the killer with a blank face, he fills in his own features. Then we follow him through a series of abortive attempts to satisfy his lusts. His struggle is interior, as was Becker's; but Lang finds means to depict the struggle visually: the look on his face, an argument with his mother, the scrawled message.

His exterior struggle is with the police and the reporters who are trying to chase him down. This is a curious struggle, unlike any other Lang created on the screen. This is both a struggle and a surrender. He both wants to be caught and to escape. He wants to be stopped but he does not turn himself in. He leaves a clue but he runs when his chasers close in.

These struggles both within and without the killer are only part of the suspense. Acting like a frame around the thriller parts of the film are the struggles among the newspaper corps that is attempting to solve the murders. The first of these struggles actually becomes the focal point of the film. Walter Kyne takes over control of a news empire from his father and conceives of means to control the men under him even though he is an incompetent playboy. He challenges the chief of each of his bureaus (television, wire service, and newspaper) to find the killer. The reward for a scoop is to be the new position of executive director. The infighting among the men and their supporters actually gives the film a cutting edge that the acting of John Barrymore, Jr., had failed to give to the struggle of the killer.

Mixed in with this struggle is that of Ed Mobley, the first-class reporter who claims not to aspire to an administrative position but who does have a Pulitzer Prize to his credit. He is the man who ultimately confronts the killer and chases him down, but his personal struggles with his profession seem more central to his character. He knows that his friend John Griffin, the newspaperman, is best suited for the position in the contest, but he refuses to become directly involved. And then he sets up his own girl friend as a potential victim for the killer in order to scoop the other reporters and the police. He succumbs rather easily to the advances of the sexy girl friend of one of the three candidates, who believes that Ed's support can be bought with favors. In the end, however, he does all the right things—helps his friend and marries the right girl. As with Dave Bannion and Jeff Warren, his good instincts dominate and lead him out of the struggle; but this comparison indicates the second major problem of the film (the first being the wooden portrayal of the killer by Barrymore). Had Bannion in *The Big Heat* not responded to his good instincts he would have killed Vince and become a killer no better than those he tracked down. Had Jeff in *Human Desire* killed at Vickie's behest he too would have become a killer, reduced to the level of the husband and wife who were killing just to hide their own inadequacies. Had Ed, however, not responded to his good instincts, he would have become a lousy reporter and rotten human; but no lives would have been lost. In other words, the struggle of Ed Mobley, while very real, lacked the intensity present in Lang's other heroes in films from the same period.

Nevertheless, *While the City Sleeps* remains one of Lang's best late films. The complexity of the struggles, the smoothness of the plot, the contemporaneity of a story about newspaper ethics, and the psychology of a sex crime contribute to a film with suspense, pace, and social impact.

10

A Concluding Appraisal

FEW CRITICS HAVE ANDREW SARRIS'S BOLDNESS in attempting to rank the most important filmmakers. Sarris put Fritz Lang into the pantheon of directors along with Griffith, Hitchcock, and eleven more.[1] Regardless, however, of the criteria the critic uses or the critic's willingness to make judgments about the relative worth of artists, Fritz Lang must be considered a filmmaker worth encountering. Looking back over a career that touched six decades and produced thirty-nine films (counting the two-part films as a single production), I believe it fair to judge Lang a flawed genius. He made films of great power and substance, films that leave an impact on the viewers. His films challenge the viewers' intellects and remain visually appealing. But often his taste or working conditions let him down and permitted him to strain an image or oversentimentalize an idea. These flaws stand out from his strengths like a weed among roses, detracting from the flowers but at the same time heightening their beauty through contrast.

The flaws in Lang's films are important because they cause strange reactions in contemporary audiences. Viewers today laugh where Lang did not intend a laugh (at Siegfried's death, for instance) or challenge the premise when Lang wanted understanding (the heart uniting the brains and the hands at the end of *Metropolis*). Lang sometimes permits his sentimentality and ideology to intrude upon his plots, forcing awkward moments, such as the conclusions of *Metropolis* and *You Only Live Once*. Rarely are such moments totally wrong. The idea may well be justified by the actions which lead up to the moment; it is usually the presentation of the idea in an overdone image—such as the flag waving at the end of *American Guerrilla*—that is flawed.

The strengths of Lang as a filmmaker far outweigh the weaknesses. Even though many actors and studio bosses disliked or misun-

169

derstood Lang, he was able to get performances from the actors that were the best of which several were capable. Peter Lorre, Randolph Scott, and Gloria Grahame created some of their best roles for Lang, as did Glenn Ford and Rudolph Klein-Rogge. Even Henry Fonda, whose comments about Lang's treatment of his actors are widely publicized,[2] was rarely better than he was in *You Only Live Once*. Lang was a perfectionist; he would rehearse at length and shoot scenes over and over until he was satisfied. But he got results, and the reputations of numerous actors have been enhanced by his direction.

Lang, like Aeschylus and Shakespeare, was expert at creating the atmosphere of tragedy. He knew how to find the right visuals to establish a tone of horror that anticipated violence and the dark struggle. The vastness of the land at the opening of *Western Union*, the documentary footage at the beginning of both *Clash by Night* and *Human Desire*, and the suicide in the first scene of *The Big Heat* testify to this talent. But perhaps the most significant creation of atmosphere came in the establishing shots at the beginning of *Siegfried*. We see Siegfried in the forest, dwarfed by the gigantic trees, demonstrating the slightness of humans when compared to all that surrounds them.

In a similar manner Lang knew the technique for developing suspense. Through the careful control of pace, selected editing, and misdirection, Lang was able to create anticipation of action. In *Scarlet Street* Professor Wanley goes to get his car to take the body of his victim to the country. First he is stopped by the police for failing to turn his headlights on, then he almost bumps into another tenant while carrying the corpse out of the apartment. Then he calls attention to himself at the toll booth by dropping his coin, and he almost runs a red light right in front of a policeman. These narrow brushes with discovery are presented through flickering and dim lights on a dark and rainy night. Altogether the images strain reality. Wanley seems too nervous, too careless; but everything that he does reminds us of his humanity. He is a rather ordinary man caught in an extraordinary situation. His foibles are those of Everyman and anticipate his eventual failure.

Many directors are capable of finding lovely sunsets or landscapes to photograph, but Lang is without equal in finding or building architecturally designed sets in which to place his characters in order to reveal and heighten the characters' struggles. No other filmmaker combines Lang's training as architect and painter, which led him to frame his characters against buildings and within sets in such a way as to depict visually their struggles. Specific frames, as though they were paintings, come to mind: Franz Becker in *M* running through streets that seem to be a maze symbolizing his mind, Siegfried and his vassals made to seem minute on the drawbridge outside the castle as they wait for Gunter's permission to enter, Captain Thorndike framed by the subway tunnel in *Man Hunt*.

Lang's value as a mythologizer is probably underestimated. When he is clearly dealing with older myths as in *Metropolis* and the Nibelungen Saga, his contribution to the mythic structure of our lives is easily understood. But Lang contributed to that structure even when he was working with different material. Consider, for example, his contributions to the concept of the American hero. He was able to make a man whom history has rendered as being murderous and unlikeable into a hero set upon doing good. In Lang's hands Frank James is a decent man, forced to do evil by an unforgiving society. Yet in *The Return of Frank James* Frank's image is not soiled by any seriously evil act; he never shoots anyone. Then in *American Guerrilla* Lang made heroic the all-American boy. Chuck Palmer represented the boys next door who had gone out to fight the war. He, too, like Frank James, was decent, good-looking, resourceful. Yet when the time came to fight, or love, he was equal to the challenge. At the extremes—one a bad man turned good, the other a good man turned soldier—Lang created characters that seem as real as the man or woman down the street, but somehow he managed to demonstrate mythic heroic qualities in them.

But perhaps most important of Lang's attributes is the worthiness of the theme that dominated his films. The dark struggles within and among his characters become statements of the dark side of our own personalities. Lang depicted struggles that represented the everyday struggles of each of us—struggles with jealousy, hate, revenge, and political and criminal tyranny. He understood how each of us is driven and confused by these conflicts. In the final analysis Fritz Lang was a first-rate entertainer who never allowed us to lose sight of his message. The dark struggle is a worthy theme, a theme that gives meaning to the visual images that dominate the films of Fritz Lang.

Notes and References

Chapter One

1. Scott Eyman, "Fritz Lang Remembered," *Take One*, 5 (March 1977), 15.

2. Perhaps the best version of the story appears in "Fritz Lang Talks about Dr. Mabuse," *Movie*, 4 (November 1962), 4–5.

Chapter Two

1. Peter Bogdanovich, *Fritz Lang in America* (New York, 1967), p. 129.

2. Nicholas Bartlett, "The Dark Struggle," *Film*, No. 32 (Summer 1962), 11.

3. "Fritz Lang Talks about the Problems of Life Today," *Film and Filming*, 8 (1962), 20.

4. "Fritz Lang's America," *Sight and Sound*, 25 (Autumn 1965), 97.

5. "Second Line," *Film Culture*, 28 (Spring 1963), 14.

6. "The Dark Struggle," p. 11.

7. *From Caligari to Hitler* (Princeton, N. J., 1947), pp. 88–95. It should be noted that Bartlett, p. 11, quotes Lang as saying that Kracauer's thesis was "100 percent nonsense—facts twisted to fit a confected theory."

8. "Fritz Lang Talks about the Problems of Life Today," p. 20.

9. Bogdanovich, pp. 21–22.

10. Bartlett, p. 11.

11. Ibid., pp. 11–12.

12. Bartlett Cormack and Fritz Lang, *Fury* in John Gassner and Dudley Nichols, eds., *Twenty Best Film Plays* (New York, 1943), p. 580.

13. *Metropolis, a Film by Fritz Lang* (New York, 1973), p. 56. This edition does not make clear who edited the shot analysis, but it is assumed that Mr. Lang did not.

14. Ibid., p. 60. These lines are taken from the original titles in the English version of the film.

Chapter Three

1. Bogdanovich, p. 67.

2. Ibid., p. 45.

3. Paul M. Jensen, *The Cinema of Fritz Lang* (New York, 1969), 46–47.

4. "The German Films of Fritz Lang," *Penguin Film Review*, VI (April 1948), 59.

5. Bogdanovich, p. 28.

6. March 6, 1947. (All reviews from the *New York Times* are taken from The *New York Times Films Reviews*, 1913–1968 (New York, 1970).

7. *New York Times*, March 13, 1927.

8. Eisner, p. 58.

Chapter Four

1. August 24, 1925, p. 17.

2. Jensen, p. 47–48.

3. *Ibid.*, p. 53.

4. The term is from Paul Rotha, *The Film Till Now* (Middlesex, 1967), p. 124.

5. The Westerns might be an exception to this generalization because Lang saw them as the American version of *The Nibelungenlied*.

6. Kracauer, pp. 91–95.

7. Jensen, p. 54.

8. Kracauer, p. 93.

9. Ibid.

10. Lotte Eisner, *The Haunted Screen* (Berkeley, Cal. 1973), pp. 163–66. The design of these films is also discussed in Léon Barsacq, *Caligari's Cabinet and Other Grand Illusions* (Boston, 1976), pp. 31–33.

11. "How Siegfried was Produced," *New York Times*, September 6, 1925.

Chapter Five

1. Kracauer, pp. 82–84.

2. The exact length of the original version is now difficult to determine. Paul Rotha (p. 274) says that the two parts together ran to more than 17,000 feet in length. Jensen says that it took four and one-half hours to view the two parts, but Eisner, *Fritz Lang* (New York, 1977), p. 408, lists running times of 95 and 100 minutes for the two parts. According to their catalogue, Janus Films has prints that run 120 and 93 minutes.

3. "Fritz Lang Talks about Dr. Mabuse," p. 4.

4. *Ibid.*

5. Kracauer, p. 248.

6. "Fritz Lang Talks about Dr. Mabuse," p. 5.

7. "The Nine Lives of Dr. Mabuse," *Sight and Sound,* (Winter 1961–62), 44.

8. Kracauer, pp. 81–84 and 248–49, and Taylor, p. 44, discuss the similarities at greater length.

Chapter Six

1. Bogdanovich, p. 86.
2. Kracauer, pp. 218–19.
3. "Fritz Lang," *Dialogue on Film,* III, No. 5, p. 8.
4. Bogdanovich, pp. 89, 126, and Jensen, p. 95.
5. Thea von Harbou, Screenplay for *M* in Roger Manvell, ed., *Masterworks of the German Cinema* (New York, 1973), p. 173.
6. See Eisner, *Fritz Lang,* pp. 117–27; Stanley J. Solomon, *The Film Idea* (New York, 1972), pp. 193–203; and Marsha Kinder and Beverle Houston, *Close Up* (New York, 1972), pp. 58–66.
7. Bogdanovich, pp. 27–28
8. D.W.C., "Fritz Lang Bows to Mammon," *New York Times,* June 14, 1936, and Bogdanovich, pp. 30–31.
9. Frank S. Nugent, "Fury," *New York Times,* June 6, 1936, and "Fury," *Time,* June 8, 1936, both reprinted in Don Whittemore and Philip Alan Cecchettini, *Passport to Hollywood* (New York, 1976), pp. 476–78.
10. Otis Ferguson, "Hollywood Half a Loaf," *New Republic,* June 10, 1936, reprinted in Whittemore and Cecchettini, pp. 473–76. Also see for similar comments, Kenneth Fearing, "Fury: Anti-lynch Film," *New Masses,* June 16, 1936, and Robert Giroux, "Unsettled Accounts," *Nation,* June 24, 1936, also both in Whittemore and Cecchettini.
11. "Fritz Lang's America," *Sight and Sound,* 25 (Summer 1955), 20.
12. April 1937 reprinted in Stanley Hochman, ed., *A Library of Film Criticism* (New York, 1974), p. 247.
13. "You Only Live Once," *New York Times,* February 1, 1937.
14. "European Director Makes Study of American Crime," *Newsweek,* January 30, 1937, p. 20, and "You Only Live Once," *Time,* January 11, 1937, p. 56.
15. "On the Deadline," *Newsweek,* September 10, 1956, p. 104; Bosley Crowther, "Beyond a Reasonable Doubt," *New York Times,* September 14, 1956, p. 27; and Arthur Knight, "SR Goes to the Movies," *Saturday Review,* September 29, 1956, p. 22.
16. Bogdanovich, pp. 35–38.
17. As quoted in Warren French, *Filmguide to the Grapes of Wrath* (Bloomington, Indiana, 1973), p. 61.

Chapter Seven

1. *The Western* (New York, 1975), p. 99.
2. Bogdanovich, p. 40.
3. "Film Directors at Work," *Theatre Arts,* 25 (March 1941), 231.
4. Jensen, p. 129.
5. Bogdanovich, pp. 39–40.
6. "Fritz Lang Changes His Mind," *New York Herald Tribune,* August

11, 1940, IV, 3, and "The Return of Frank James," *New York Herald Tribune*, August 10, 1940, p. 6.

    7. "The Return of Frank James," p. 6.

    8. George N. Fenin and William K. Everson, *The Western* (New York, 1962), pp. 241–42.

    9. Jon Tuska, *The Filming of the West* (Garden City, N.Y., 1976), pp. 362–63.

    10. *Zane Grey* (New York, 1973), pp. 82–83.

    11. Bogdanovich, p. 45.

    12. Ibid., p. 46.

    13. Ibid.

    14. Ibid., pp. 79–80.

    15. See for example Andrew Sarris, *The American Cinema* (New York, 1968), pp. 64–65.

    16. *New York Times*, May 15, 1952.

    17. "Rancho Notorious," *New York World Telegraph and Sun*, May 15, 1952, as reprinted in Hockman, p. 251.

Chapter Eight

    1. Kracauer, p. 150.

    2. Bogdanovich, p. 57.

    3. The creation of the set for this scene is described in Bogdanovich, pp. 57–59.

    4. Jensen, pp. 151–52.

    5. *Interviews with Film Directors* (New York, 1967), p. 309.

    6. James Robert Parish and Michael R. Pitts, *The Great Spy Pictures* (Metuchen, N.J., 1974), p. 304.

    7. Bogdanovich, pp. 69–70.

    8. Parish and Pitts, p. 112.

    9. Bogdanovich, p. 73.

    10. Ibid., pp. 70–71.

    11. Ibid., p. 75.

    12. Actually the French filmmakers who developed the concept of *film noir* learned much from Lang and have been partly responsible for keeping his reputation high.

Chapter Nine

    1. "Fritz Lang's America," *Sight and Sound*, 25 (Fall 1955), 94.

    2. "Happily Ever After," *Penguin Film Review*, 5 (January 1948), 28.

    3. *Fritz Lang*, p. 247.

    4. *Fritz Lang*, pp. 255–56.

    5. Bogdanovich, p. 67. The film was banned in New York in what the *New*

York Times (January 5, 1946) called "one of the most drastic actions ever taken by the New York State Board of Censors."

6. *Fritz Lang*, pp. 264–65.
7. Bogdanovich, p. 84.
8. Ibid., pp. 85–86.
9. *Fritz Lang*, p. 343.
10. Ibid., p. 341.
11. Ibid., p. 351.
12. Bogdanovich, pp. 102–106.

Chapter Ten

1. *The American Cinema*, pp. 63–65.
2. Gary Arnold, "Film Director Fritz Lang Dies," *Washington Post*, August 4, 1976, p. 36.

Selected Bibliography

BOOKS

BARSACQ, LEON. *Caligari's Cabinet and Other Grand Illusions.* Revised and edited by Elliott Stein. Boston: New York Graphic Society, 1976. A study of set design that devotes considerable space to Lang's German films.

BOGDANOVICH, PETER. *Fritz Lang in America.* New York: Praeger, 1967. A younger director interviews an older one and the result provides Lang's most detailed analysis of his American films.

EISNER, LOTTE H. *Fritz Lang.* New York: Oxford University Press, 1977. Written by a woman who is both a perceptive critic and longtime friend of the director, this book is the most important single study of his films. A chapter is devoted to each film; other chapters deal with his working methods and style.

———. *The Haunted Screen.* Berkeley: University of California Press, 1973. This is the classic study of expressionism in German cinema and includes considerable discussion of Lang.

VON HARBOU, THEA. *Metropolis.* Boston: Gregg, 1975. The novel version of the movie. No one today seems to know for certain whether the novel was written before, during, or after the making of the film.

JENSEN, PAUL M. *The Cinema of Fritz Lang.* New York: A. S. Barnes and Co., 1969. A full-length study that is better on the history of Lang's films than on analysis. In one way or another Jensen does cover all of Lang's films.

KRACAUER, SIEGFRIED. *From Caligari to Hitler.* Princeton, N.J.: Princeton University Press, 1947. This famous psychological study of German films places Lang in the milieu that led to Hitler. Kracauer's thesis is well argued, but Lang did not think much of the book.

LANG, FRITZ, and THEA VON HARBOU. *Metropolis.* New York: Simon and Schuster, 1973. This is a shot analysis for *Metropolis* with the addition of the titles from the English version of the film and excerpts from the novel by the same name by von Harbou. The names of the translators and editors of this book are not given.

PARTS OF BOOKS

VON HARBOU, THEA. *M* in *Masterworks of the German Cinema*, ed. Roger
    Manvell. New York: Harper & Row, 1973, pp. 97–177. Screenplay for
    M.
LANG, FRITZ. "The Freedom of the Screen" in *Hollywood Directors,
    1941–1976*, ed. Richard Koszarski. New York: Oxford University Press,
    1977, pp. 134–42. In this essay, which originally appeared in *Theatre
    Arts* (December 1947), Lang cries out against censorship of movies.
———. "Fritz Lang Seminar" in *Dialogue on Film: Fritz Lang/Bernardo
    Bertolucci*, ed. Rochelle Reed. Beverly Hills, Cal.: the American Film
    Institute, 1974, pp. 2–13. An interview with Lang conducted at the
    AFI's Center for Advanced Film Studies.
———, and BARTLETT CORMACK. *Fury* in *Twenty Best Film Plays*, ed. John
    Gassner and Dudley Nichols. New York: Crown Publishers, 1943, pp.
    521–82. Screenplay for *Fury*.
SARRIS, ANDREW. "Fritz Lang" in *The American Cinema*. New York: E. P.
    Dutton, 1968, pp. 63–65. Interesting short essay in which Sarris places
    Lang in his pantheon of film directors.
SHIVAS, MARK. "Interview with Fritz Lang" in *Interviews with Film Di-
    rectors*, ed. Andrew Sarris. New York: Avon, 1967, pp. 309–15. An
    interesting interview concentrating on Mabuse, with notes and filmog-
    raphy added by Sarris.
SOLOMAN, STANLEY J. *M* in *The Classic Cinema*. New York: Harcourt,
    Brace, Jovanovich, 1973, pp. 129–48. This chapter includes an over-
    view by Soloman, selections from the books by Kracauer and Jensen,
    and an essay by Eric Rhode, "Fritz Lang (the German Period)" from
    Tower of Babel: Speculations on the Cinema by Rhode.
WELLS, H. G. "The Silliest Film: Will Machinery Make Robots of Men" in
    Authors on Film, ed. Harry M. Geduld. Bloomington: Indiana Univer-
    sity Press, 1972, pp. 59–67. An attack on *Metropolis*.
WHITTENMORE, DON, and PHILIP ALAN CECCHETTINI. "Fritz Lang" in
    Passport to Hollywood. New York: McGraw-Hill, 1976, pp. 442–95.
    This chapter includes the authors' overview of Lang's career, Lam-
    bert's two part essay, and a series of reviews of *Fury*.

PERIODICALS

BARLETT, NICHOLAS. "The Dark Struggle," *Film*, 32 (Summer 1962),
    11–13. A good analysis of Lang's films that suggested the theme of this
    present study. Includes an interview.
BERG, GRETCHEN. "Fritz Lang—'Contempt,'" *Take One*, 2 (1968), 12–13.
    An interview with Lang about his work as an actor in Godard's film.
EISNER, LOTTE H. "The German Films of Fritz Lang," *Penguin Film Re-
    view*, 6 (April 1948), 53–61. Lang's most perceptive critic gives some
    firsthand impressions of his early films.

EYMAN, SCOTT. "Fritz Lang Remembered," *Take One*, 5 (March 1977), 15–16. An old friend reminisces just after Lang's death about his last years.

HART, HENRY. "Fritz Lang Today," *Films in Review*, 7 (1956), 261–63. An article based on an interview in which Lang "gently deprecates some of his past," especially *Metropolis*.

LAMBERT, GAVIN. "Fritz Lang's America, Part I," *Sight and Sound*, 25 (Summer 1925), 15–21, 55. An important study of Lang's American films which suggests a decline of Lang's ability under the Hollywood system. Lambert says Lang became less "personal."

————. "Fritz Lang's America, Part II," *Sight and Sound*, 25 (Autumn 1955), 92–97.

LANG, FRITZ. "Fritz Lang Talks About Dr. Mabuse," *Movie*, 4, (November 1962), 4–5. Lang discusses the history of all three of his Mabuse films, with special attention on the last one.

————. "Fritz Lang Talks About the Problems of Life Today," *Films and Filming*, 8 (1962), 20–21. Lang on society and films.

————. "Happily Ever After," *Penguin Film Review*, 5 (January 1948), 22–29. Lang discusses the importance of a happy ending, especially in light of the controversy over the ending of *Woman in the Window*.

TAYLOR, JOHN RUSSELL. "The Nine Lives of Dr. Mabuse," *Sight and Sound*, 31 (Winter 1961–62), 43–46. A useful analysis of Lang's last film as the final step in a progression that began early in his career.

Filmography

Note: Dates given with the production company are those of the first release of the film. Since the exact release dates are not always known, the dates of the first reviews in the *New York Times* have been included to establish approximate dates where necessary. (These reviews are reprinted in *New York Times Film Reviews, 1913–1968*. New York: Arno Press, 1970.) Running times listed are those of prints as they are distributed in the United States today; occasionally, especially for the German films, these times differ somewhat from those of the films as originally released. 8mm. and 16mm. prints of most of Lang's major silent German films and some of his American talking pictures are legally available for sale from these distributors of films for home use:

Blackhawk Films, P.O. Box 3990, Davenport, Iowa 52808

Niles Film Products, Inc., 1141 Mishawaka Ave., South Bend, Indiana 46615.

Reel Images, 456 Monroe Turnpike, Monroe, Conn. 06468.

Thunderbird Films, P.O. Box 65157, Los Angeles, Cal. 90065.

HALBBLUT (HALF CASTE) (Decla-Bioscop, 1919)*
Screenplay: Fritz Lang
Photography: Carl Hoffmann
Cast: Ressel Orla, Carl de Vogt, Gilda Langer, Carl-Gerrard Schroder, Paul Morgan
Running Time: Unknown
Premiere: Early April 1919. Marmorhaus, Berlin
*For further available technical information about this and other German silent films, consult Gerhard Lamprecht, ed., *Deutsche Stummfilme*. 9 Vol. Berlin: Deutsche Kinemathek, 1968–70.

DER HERR DER LIEBE (THE MASTER OF LOVE) (Decla-Bioscop/ Helios Film, 1919)
Screenplay: Oscar Koffler
Photography: Emil Schünemann
180

Cast: Carl de Vogt (Disescu), Gilda Langer (Yvette), Erika Unruh, Fritz Lang
Running time: Approximately 58 minutes (1,316 meters long)
Premiere: Mid-September 1919, Richard Oswald Lichtspiele, Berlin

DIE SPINNEN (THE SPIDERS). Part One: **DER GOLDENE SEE (THE GOLDEN LAKE)** (Decla-Bioscop, 1919)
Screenplay: Fritz Lang
Photography: Emil Schünemann
Art Direction: Otto Hunte, Carl Ludwig Kirmse, Hermann Warm, Heinrich Umlauff
Cast: Carl de Vogt (Kai Hoog), Ressel Orla (Lio Sha), Lil Dagover (Priestess of the Sun King)
Running time: Approximately 81 minutes (1,900 meters long)
Premiere: October 3, 1919, Richard Oswald Lichtspiele, Berlin

HARA–KARI (Decla-Bioscop, 1919)
Screenplay: Max Jungk (from the play *Madame Butterfly*, by John Luther Long and David Belasco)
Photography: Max Fassbaender
Art Direction: Heinrich Umlauff
Cast: Paul Biensfeldt (Daimyo Tokuyawa), Lil Dagover (O-Take-San), Georg John (Buddist Monk), Meinhard Maur (Prince Matahari), Rudolph Lettinger (Karan), Erner Hübsch (Kin-Be-Araki), Kaete Jüster (Hanake), Nils Prien (Olaf J. Anderson), Herta Heden (Eva), Loni Nest
Running time: Approximately 108 minutes (2,525 meters long)
Premiere: Late December 1919, Marmorhaus, Berlin

DIE SPINNEN. Part Two: **DAS BRILLANTEN SCHIFF (THE DIAMOND SHIP)** (Decla-Bioscop, 1920)
Screenplay: Fritz Lang
Photography: Karl Freund
Art Direction: Otto Hunte, Karl Ludwig Kirmse, Hermann Warm, Heinrich Unlauff
Cast: Carl de Vogt, Ressel Orla, Lil Dagover, Paul Morgan, Friedrich Kuehne, Georg John, Meinhardt Maur, Gilda Langer, Paul Biensfeldt
Running time: Approximately 95 minutes (2,219 meters long)
Premiere: Early February 1920. Theater am Moritzblatz, Berlin

DAS WANDERNDE BILD (THE WANDERING IMAGE) (Joe May Company, 1920)
Screenplay: Fritz Lang, Thea von Harbou
Cast: Mia May, Hans Marr, Rudolf Klein-Rohden, Harry Frank, Loni Nest
Running time: Approximately 87 minutes (2,032 meters long)
Premiere: December, 25, 1920, Tauentzienpalast, Berlin

VIER UM DIE FRAU (FOUR AROUND A WOMAN) (Decla-Bioscop, 1920)
Screenplay: Fritz Lang, Thea von Harbou
Cast: Carola Trölle (Madame Yquem), Ludwig Hartau (Mr. Yquem), Anton Edthofer (The Swindler), Rudolph Klein-Rogge.
Running time: unknown
Premiere: Early February 1920, Marmorhaus, Berlin

DER MÜDE TOD (THE WEARY DEATH). American/British title: **DESTINY.** (Decla-Bioscop, 1921)
Screenplay: Fritz Lang, Thea von Harbou
Photography: Erich Nietzschmann, Fritz Arno Wagner, Hermann Saalfrank
Lighting: Robert Hegerwald
Art Direction: Hermann Warm, Robert Herlth, Walter Röhrig
Cast: Bernhard Goetzke (Death), Lil Dagover (Young Woman), Walter Janssen (Young Man), Rudolph Klein-Rogge (Girolamo)
Running Time: c. 125 minutes
Premiere: October 7, 1921, Mozartsaal and U.T. Kürfurste Kürfurstendamm, Berlin
American Premiere: July 1923 under the title *Between Two Worlds*
16mm. Rental: Kit Parker, Museum of Modern Art, and others
16mm. Sales: Reel Images

DR. MABUSE, DER SPIELER (DR. MABUSE, THE GAMBLER). (Part One: **DR. MABUSE, DER SPIELER—EIN BILD DER ZEIT (DR. MABUSE, THE GAMBLER—A PICTURE OF THE TIME).** Part Two: **INFERNO—MENSCHEN DER ZEIT (INFERNO—MEN OF THE TIME)** (Ullstein-Uco Film-Decla-Bioscop-Ufa)
Screenplay: Fritz Lang, Thea von Harbou, from a novel by Norbert Jacques
Photography: Carl Hoffmann
Art Direction: Otto Hunte, Stahl-Urach
Cast: Rudolph Klein-Rogge (Mabuse), Alfred Abel (Count Told), Aud Egede Nissen (Cara Carozza), Gertrude Welcker (Countess Told), Bernhard Goetzke (Von Wenck), Paul Richter (Edgar Hull)
Running Time: Janus Prints—(Mabuse) 120 minutes (Inferno) 93 minutes
Premiere: *(Mabuse)* April 27, 1922 *(Inferno)* May 26, 1922, Ufa Palast am Zoo, Berlin
American Premiere: Unknown (first reviewed by the *New York Times* August 9, 1927)
16mm. Rental: Janus
8 and 16mm. Sales: A condensed version, cut from the two original films for American release, is available from Thunderbird Films. Uncut versions of both parts are sold by Reel Images

DIE NIBELUNGEN. Part One: **SIEGFRIEDS TOD (DEATH OF SIEGFRIED).** Part Two: **KRIEMHILDS RACHE (KRIEMHILD'S REVENGE)** (Decla-Bioscop-Ufa, 1924)

Screenplay: Fritz Lang and Thea von Harbou, based on *Die Nibelungen* and Norse Sagas

Photography: Carl Hoffmann, Günther Rittau, and Walter Ruttmann (for the animated "Dream of the Falcon" sequence)

Art Direction: Otto Hunte, Erich Kettelhut, Carl Vollbrecht

Costumes: Paul Gerd Guderian, Anne Willkomm

Armor and Weapons of the Huns: Heinrich Umlauff

Makeup: Otto Genath

Music: Gottfried Huppertz

Cast: Paul Richter (Siegfried), Margarete Schön (Kriemhild), Rudolph Klein-Rogge (Etzel, King of the Huns), Georg August Koch (Hildebrand), Theodor Loos (Gunther), Bernhard Goetzke (Volker von Alzey), Hans Adalbert von Schlettow (Hagen Tronje), Georg John (Mime Alberich, I; Blaodel, II), Gertrude Arnold (Queen Ute), Hanna Ralph (Brunhild), Rudolph Rittner (Rüdiger), Fritz Albert (Dietrich)

Running Time: Kit Parker Prints: (*Siegfried*) 130 minutes, (*Kriemhild's Revenge*) 90 minutes

Premiere: (*Siegfried*) February 14, 1924 (*Kriemhild's Rache*) April 26, 1924 Ufa Palast am Zoo, Berlin

American Premiere: (*Siegfried*) August 23, 1925 (first reviewed by the *New York Times*, August 24, 1925); (*Kriemhild's Revenge*) Fall 1928 (first reviewed by the *New York Times*, October 16, 1928)

16mm. Rentals: Kit Parker, Museum of Modern Art, and others

8 and 16mm. Sales: Blackhawk Films

METROPOLIS (Ufa, 1927)

Screenplay: Fritz Lang, Thea von Harbou

Photography: Karl Freund, Günther Rittau

Special Effects Photography: Eugene Schüfftan

Art Direction: Otto Hunte, Erich Kettelhut, Carl Vollbrecht

Sculptures: Walter Schultze-Middendorff

Music: Gottfried Huppertz

Cast: Brigitte Helm (Maria), Alfred Abel (John Federson), Gustave Fröhlich (Freder Frederson), Rudolph Klein-Rogge (Rotwang), Heinrich George (Foreman), Fritz Rasp (Grot)

Running Time: MOMA Print—133 minutes

Premiere: January 10, 1927, Ufa Palast am Zoo, Berlin

American Premiere: Spring, 1927 (First reviewed by the *New York Times*, March 7, 1927)

16mm. Rentals: Kit Parker, Museum of Modern Art, and others

8 and 16mm. Sales: Niles Film Products, Reel Images, Thunderbird Films

SPIONE (SPIES) (Fritz Lang-Film-G.M.B.H., released by Ufa, 1928)
Producer: Fritz Lang
Screenplay: Fritz Lang, Thea von Harbou
Photography: Fritz Arno Wagner
Art Direction: Otto Hunte, Carl Vollbrecht
Music: Werner R. Heymann
Cast: Rudolph Klein-Rogge (Haighi), Gerda Maurus (Sonja), Willy Fritsch
   (Detective), Lupu Pick (Masimoto), Fritz Rasp (Ivan Stepanov), Lien
   Deyers (Kitty)
Running Time: MOMA Print—85 minutes
Premiere: March 22, 1928, Ufa Palast am Zoo, Berlin
American Premiere: January 15, 1929 (first reviewed by the *New York
   Times*, May 20, 1928, and again, March 5, 1929)
16mm. Rental: Kit Parker, Museum of Modern Art, and others
8 and 16mm. Sales: Blackhawk Films

FRAU IM MOND (WOMAN IN THE MOON) (Fritz-Lang-Film-
   G.M.B.H., released by Ufa, 1929)
Producer: Fritz Lang
Screenplay: Fritz Lang, Thea von Harbou
Photography: Curt Courant, Oskar Fischinger, Otto Kanturek
Special Effects: Konstantin Tschetwerikoff
Art Direction: Otto Hunte, Emil Hasler, Carl Vollbrecht
Backdrop Photographs: Horst von Harbou
Music: Willy Schimdt-Gentner
Technical Advisors: Hermann Oberth, Willy Ley
Cast: Gerda Maurus (Frieda Venten), Willy Fritsch (Professor Helius),
   Fritz Rasp (Walt Turner), Gustav von Wangenheim (Hans Windegger),
   Klaus Pohl (Professor Georg Manfeldt), Gustl Stark-Gstettenbaur (Gus-
   tav)
Running Time: Kit Parker Print—156 minutes
Premiere: October 15, 1929, Ufa Palast am Zoo, Berlin
American Premiere: February 6, 1931
16mm. Rental: Kit Parker and others
16mm. Sales: Reel Images

M (NERO Film A.G.-Ver. Star Film-G.M.B.H., 1931)
Producer: Seymour Nebenzal
Screenplay: Fritz Lang, Thea von Harbou
Photography: Fritz Arno Wagner, Gustav Rathje
Camera Operator: Karl Vash
Art Direction: Carl Vollbrecht, Emil Hasler
Backdrop Photographs: Horst von Harbou

Music: excerpts from *Peer Gynt* by Edvard Grieg ("murderer's theme" whistled by Fritz Lang)
Sound: Adolf Jansen
Sound Editor: Paul Falkenberg
Cast: Peter Lorre (Franz Becker), Otto Wernicke (Karl Lohmann), Gustav Gründgens (Schraenker), Theo Lingen (Baurenfaenger), Theodor Loos (Commissioner Groeber), Georg John (Peddler), Ellen Widmann (Madame Becker), Inge Landgut (Elsie), Ernst Stahl-Nachbaur (Police Chief), Paul Kemp (Pickpocket), Franz Stein (Minister), Rudolf Blümner (Attorney)
Running Time: Janus Print—99 minutes
Premiere: May 11, 1931, Ufa Palast am Zoo, Berlin
American Premiere: Spring 1933 (first reviewed by the *New York Times*, July 19, 1931 and again, April 3, 1933)
16mm. Rental: Janus and others
8 and 16mm. Sales: Niles Films; Reel Images

DAS TESTAMENT VON DR. MABUSE/LA TESTAMENT DU DR. MABUSE (THE LAST WILL OF DR. MABUSE) (Nero Film-Constantin-Deutsche Universal, 1933)
Producer: Fritz Lang
Screenplay: Fritz Lang, Thea von Harbou, based on characters from a novel by Norbert Jacques
Photography: Fritz Arno Wagner, Karl Vash
Art Direction: Carl Vollbrecht, Emil Hasler
Music: Dr. Hans Erdmann
Cast: Rudolph Klein-Rogge (Mabuse), Oskar Beregi (Dr. Baum), Karl Meixner (Landlord), Theodor Loos (Dr. Kramm), Otto Wernicke (Karl Lohmann), Klaus Pohl (Müller), Wera Liessem (Lilli), Gustav Diessl (Kent)
Running Time: Janus print—120 minutes
Premiere: Probably 1933 in France
American Premiere: (English Language Version) Winter 1943 (first reviewed by the *New York Times*, March 20, 1943)
16mm. Rental: Janus and Budget
16mm. Sales: Reel Images, as *The Crime of Dr. Mabuse*

LILIOM (S.A.F.-Fox Europa, 1934)
Producer: Erich Pommer
Assistant Director: Jacques P. Feydeau
Screenplay: Fritz Lang, Robert Liebmann, Bernard Zimmer, based on the play by Ferenc Molnar
Photography: Rudolph Maté, Louis Née

Art Direction: Paul Colin, René Renoux
Music: Jean Lenoir, Franz Waxman
Cast: Charles Boyer (Liliom), Madeleine Ozeray (Julie), Florelle (Madame
  Muskat), Robert Arnoux (Strong Arm)
Running Time: 120 minutes
Premiere: May 15, 1934, Paris
American Premiere: March 16, 1935 (first reviewed by the *New York Times*,
  March 8, 1935)

FURY (Metro-Goldwyn-Mayer, 1936)
Producer: Joseph L. Mankiewicz
Assistant Director: Horace Hough
Screenplay: Fritz Lang and Bartlett Cormack, based on the story "Mob
  Rule" by Norman Krasna
Photography: Joseph Ruttenberg
Art Direction: Cedric Gibbons (assisted by William A. Horning, Edwin B.
  Willis)
Costumes: Dolly Tree
Music: Franz Waxman
Editor: Frank Sullivan
Cast: Spencer Tracy (Joe Wheeler), Sylvia Sidney (Katherine Grant), Wal-
  ter Abel (District Attorney), Bruce Cabot (Kirby Dawson), Edward Ellis
  (Sheriff), Walter Brennan (Bugs Mayers)
Running Time: 94 minutes
Premiere: June 5, 1936 (first reviewed by the *New York Times*, June 6,
  1936)
16mm. Rental: Films, Inc.

YOU ONLY LIVE ONCE (Wanger–United Artists, 1937)
Producer: Walter Wanger
Assistant Director: Robert Lee
Writers: Gene Towne, Graham Baker, based on a story by Towne
Photography: Leon Shamroy
Art Direction: Alexander Toluboff
Music: Alfred Newman. Song "A Thousand Dreams of You" by Louis Alter,
  Paul Francis Webster
Editor: Daniel Mandell
Cast: Sylvia Sidney (Jo Graham), Henry Fonda (Eddie Taylor), Barton
  MacLane (Stephen Whitney), Jean Dixon (Bonnie Graham), William
  Gargan (Father Dolan)
Running Time: Audio-Brandon print—85 minutes
Premiere: January 29, 1937 (first reviewed by the *New York Times*, Feb-
  ruary 1, 1937)
16mm. Rental: Audio-Brandon and Budget
Super-8mm. Sales:-Reel Images

YOU AND ME (Paramount, 1938)
Screenplay: Virginia Van Upp, based on a story by Norman Krasna
Photography: Charles Lang, Jr.
Art Direction: Hans Dreier, Ernest Fegté
Set Decoration: A. E. Freudeman
Music: Kurt Weill, Boris Morros
Songs: "The Right Guy for Me" by Weill, Sam Coslow: "You and Me" by
Ralph Freed, Frederick Hollander
Musical Advisor: Phil Boutelie
Editor: Paul Weatherwax
Cast: Sylvia Sidney (Helen Roberts), George Raft (Joe Dennis), Robert
Cummings (Jim), Barton MacLane (Mickey)
Running Time: 94 minutes
Premiere: June 3, 1938 (first reviewed by the *New York Times*, June 2,
1938)
16mm. Rental: Universal 16

THE RETURN OF FRANK JAMES (Twentieth Century-Fox, 1940)
Producer: Darryl F. Zanuck
Associate Producer: Kenneth Macgowan
Screenplay: Sam Hellman
Photography (Technicolor): George Barnes, William V. Skall
Art Direction: Richard Day, Wiard B. Ihnen
Set Decoration: Thomas Little
Costumes: Travis Banton
Music: David Buttolph
Editor: Walter Thompson
Cast: Henry Fonda (Frank James), Gene Tierney (Eleanor), Jackie Cooper
(Clem), Henry Hull (Major Rufus Todd), J. Edward Bromberg (George
Rynyan) John Carradine (Bob Ford)
Running Time: 94 minutes
Premiere: August 16, 1940 (first reviewed by the *New York Times*, August
10, 1940)
16mm. Rental: Budget and others

WESTERN UNION (Twentieth Century-Fox, 1941)
Associate Producer: Harry Joe Brown
Screenplay: Robert Carson, based on a novel by Zane Grey
Photography (Technicolor): Edward Cronjager, Allen M. Davey
Art Direction: Richard Day, Wiard B. Ihnen
Set Decoration: Thomas Little
Costumes: Travis Banton
Music: David Buttolph
Editor: Robert Bischoff

Cast: Robert Young (Richard Blake), Randolph Scott (Vance Shaw), Dean
    Jagger (Edward Creighton), Virginia Gilmore (Sue Creighton), John Car-
    radine (Don Murdoch), Slim Summerville (Herman), Chill Wills
    (Homer), Barton McLane (Jack Slade)
Running Time: 90 minutes
Premiere: February 21, 1941 (first reviewed by the *New York Times*, Feb-
    ruary 7, 1941)
16mm. Rental: Films, Inc.

MAN HUNT (Twentieth Century–Fox, 1941)
Associate Producer: Kenneth Macgowan
Screenplay: Dudley Nichols, based on the novel *Rogue Male* by Geoffrey
    Household
Photography: Arthur Miller
Art Direction: Richard Day, Wiard B. Ihnen
Set Decoration: Thomas Little
Costumes: Travis Banton
Music: Alfred Newman
Editor: Allen McNeil
Cast: Walter Pidgeon (Captain Thorndike), Joan Bennett (Jenny), George
    Sanders (Quive-Smith), John Carradine (Mr. Jones), Roddy McDowall
    (Vaner)
Running Time: 105 minutes
Premiere: June 20, 1941 (first reviewed by the *New York Times*, June 14,
    1941)
16mm. Rental: Films, Inc.

HANGMEN ALSO DIE! (Arnold Productions-United Artists, 1943)
Executive Producer: Arnold Pressburger
Associate Producer: T. W. Baumfield
Assistant Directors: Archie Mayo, Fred Pressburger
Screenplay: Fritz Lang, Bertolt Brecht, John Wexley, based on a story by
    Lang and Brecht
Photography: James Wong Howe
Art Direction: William Darling
Costumes: Julie Heron
Music: Hanns Eisler
Song: "No Surrender" by Eisler, Sam Coslow
Editor: Gene Fowler, Jr.
Production Manager: Carl Harriman
Cast: Brian Donlevy (Franz Svoboda), Walter Brennan (Professor
    Novotny), Anna Lee (Mascha Novotny), Gene Lockhart (Emil Czaka),
    Dennis O'Keefe (Jan Horek), Alexander Granach (Alois Gruber), Mar-
    garet Wycherly (Ludmilla Novotny)

Running Time: 123 minutes
Premiere: March 26, 1943 (first reviewed by the *New York Times*, April 16, 1943)
16mm. Rental: Budget

MINISTRY OF FEAR (Paramount, 1944)
Producer: Seton I. Miller
Assistant Director: George Templeton
Screenplay: Seton I. Miller, based on the novel by Graham Greene
Photography: Henry Sharp
Art Direction: Hans T. Dreier, Hal Pereia
Set Decoration: Bert Granger
Music: Victor Young
Editor: Archie Marshek
Cast: Ray Milland (Stephen Neale), Marjorie Reynolds (Carla Hilfe), Carl Esmond (Willi Hilfe), Dan Duryea (Costa/Travers), Hilliary Brooke (Mrs. Bellane), Percy Waram (Inspector Prentice)
Running Time: 86 minutes
Premiere: October 16, 1944 (first reviewed by the *New York Times*, February 8, 1945)
16mm. Rental: Universal 16

THE WOMAN IN THE WINDOW (Christie Corporation–International Pictures, released by R.K.O. 1944) Released before, but produced after, *Ministry of Fear*
Producer: Nunnally Johnson
Assistant Director: Richard Harlan
Screenplay: Nunnally Johnson, based on the novel *Once Off Guard* by J. H. Wallis
Photography: Milton Krasner
Special Effects: Vernon Walker
Art Direction: Duncan Cramer
Set Decoration: Julia Heron
Costumes: Muriel King
Music: Arthur Lang
Editor: Marjorie Johnson
Cast: Edward G. Robinson (Richard Wanley), Joan Bennett (Alice), Raymond Massey (District Attorney), Dan Duryea (Blackmailer), Edmond Breon (Dr. Barkstone), Thomas E. Jackson (Inspector Jackson)
Running Time: 99 minutes
Premiere: October 11, 1944 (first reviewed by the *New York Times*, January 26, 1945)
16mm Rental: United Artists 16

SCARLET STREET (Diana Productions, released by Universal, 1945)
Producer: Fritz Lang
Executive Director: Walter Wanger
Assistant Director: Melville Shyer
Screenplay: Dudley Nichols, based on the novel and play *La Chienne* by
   Georges de la Fouchardière (with Mouézy-Eon)
Photography: Milton Krasner
Special Photographic Effects: John P. Fulton
Art Direction: Alexander Golitzen
Set Decoration: Russell A. Gausman, Carl Lawrence
Costumes: Travis Benton
Paintings: John Decker
Music: Hans J. Salter
Editor: Arthur Hilton
Cast: Edward G. Robinson (Chris Cross), Joan Bennett (Kitty Marsh), Dan
   Duryea (Johnny), Margaret Lindsay (Millie), Rosalind Ivan (Adele)
Running Time: 98 minutes
Premiere: December 28, 1945 (first reviewed by the *New York Times*,
   February 15, 1946)
16mm. Rental: The Movie Center
16mm. Sales: Reel Images

CLOAK AND DAGGER (United States Pictures, Inc., released by Warner
   Bros., 1946)
Producer: Milton Sperling
Assistant Director: Russ Saunders
Screenplay: Albert Maltz, Ring Lardner, Jr., based on a story by Boris
   Ingster and John Larkin, suggested by a book by Corey Ford and Alastair
   MacBain.
Photography: Sol Polita
Art Direction: Max Parker
Set Decoration: Walter Hilford
Special Effects: Harry Barndollar, Edwin DuPar
Music: Max Steiner
Editor: Christian Nyby
Technical Advisor: Michael Burke
Cast: Gary Cooper (Alvah Jesper), Lilli Palmer (Gina), Robert Alda (Pinky),
   Vladimir Sokoloff (Dr. Polda)
Running Time: 106 minutes
Premiere: September 28, 1946 (first reviewed by the *New York Times*,
   October 5, 1946)

SECRET BEYOND THE DOOR (Diana Productions, released by Univer-
   sal-International, 1948)

Producer: Fritz Lang
Executive Producer: Walter Wanger
Assistant Director: William Holland
Screenplay: Silvia Richards, based on the story "Museum Piece No. 13" by
    Rufus King
Photography: Stanley Cortez
Production Designer: Max Parker
Set Decoration: Russell A. Gausman, John Austin
Music: Miklos Rosza
Editor: Arthur Hilton
Cast: Joan Bennett (Celia Lamphere), Michael Redgrave (Mark Lamphere),
    Anne Revere (Caroline Lamphere), Barbara O'Neil (Miss Robey)
Running Time: 99 minutes
Premiere: February 1948 (first reviewed by the *New York Times*, January
    16, 1948.)
16mm. Rental: Ivy Films

HOUSE BY THE RIVER (Fidelity Pictures, released by Republic, 1950)
Producer: Howard Welsch
Associate Producer: Robert Peters
Assistant Director: John Grubbs
Screenplay: Mel Dinelli, based on a novel by A. P. Herbert
Photography: Edward Cronjager
Art Direction: Bert Leven
Set Decoration: Charles Thompson, John McCarthy, Jr.
Special Effects: Howard and Theodore Lydecker
Costumes: Adele Palmer
Music: George Antheil
Editor: Arthur D. Hilton
Production Manager: Joseph Dillpe
Cast: Louis Hayward (Stephen Byrne), Lee Bowman (John Byrne), Jane
    Wyatt (Majorie Byrne), Dorothy Patrick (Emily Gaunt)
Running Time: 88 minutes
Premiere: March 25, 1950 (first reviewed by the *New York Times*, May 2,
    1950)

AN AMERICAN GUERRILLA IN THE PHILIPPINES (Twentieth Cen-
    tury–Fox, 1950)
Producer: Lamar Trotti
Second-Unit Director: Robert D. Webb
Assistant Director: Horace Hough
Screenplay: Lamar Trotti, based on the novel of the same title by Ira
    Wolfert
Photography (Technicolor): Harry Jackson

Special Photographic Effects: Fred Sersen
Art Direction: Lyle Wheeler, J. Russell Spencer
Set Decoration: Thomas Little, Stuart Reiss
Costumes: Travilla
Music: Cyril Mockridge
Editor: Robert Simpson
Production Manager: F. E. Johnson
Cast: Tyrone Power (Chuck Palmer), Micheline Presle (Jeanne Martinez), Jack Elam (Spenser), Bob Pattern (Lovejoy), Tom Ewell (Jim Mitchell)
Running Time: 105 minutes
Premiere: December 1950 (first reviewed by the *New York Times*, November 8, 1950)
16mm. Rental: Films, Inc.

RANCHO NOTORIOUS (Fidelity Pictures, released by RKO Radio, 1952)
Producer: Howard Welsch
Assistant Director: Emmert Emerson
Screenplay: Daniel Taradash, based on the story "Gunsight Whitman" by Silvia Richards
Photography (Technicolor): Hal Mohr
Art Direction: Robert Priestly
Music: Emil Newman
Songs: "The Legend of Chuck-A-Luck" (sung by William Lee), "Gypsy Davey," "Get Away, Young Man" (sung by Marlene Dietrich) by Ken Darby
Editor: Otto Ludwig
Cast: Marlene Dietrich (Altar Keane), Arthur Kennedy (Vern Haskell), Mel Ferrer (Frenchy Fairmont), Jack Elam (Geary), Dan Seymour (Commanche Paul), George Reeves (Wilson), Gloria Henry (Beth Forbes), William Frawley (Baldy Gunder), Lisa Ferraday (Maxine), John Raven (Chuck-A-Luck Dealer)
Running Time: 89 minutes
Premiere: March 1952 (first reviewed by the *New York Times*, May 15, 1952)
16mm. Rental: United Films

CLASH BY NIGHT (Wald-Krasna Productions—RKO Radio Pictures, 1952)
Executive Producer: Jerry Wald
Producer: Harriet Parsons
Screenplay: Alfred Hayes, based on the play of the same title by Clifford Odets
Photography: Nicholas Musuraca
Special Photographic Effects: Harold Wellman

Art Direction: Albert S. D'Agostino, Carroll Clark
Set Decoration: Darrell Silvera, Jack Mills
Music: Roy Webb; song "I Hear a Rhapsody" by Dick Gasparre, Jack Baker, George Fragos (sung by Tony Martin)
Editor: George J. Amy
Cast: Barbara Stanwyck (Mae Doyle), Paul Douglas (Jerry d'Amato), Robert Ryan (Earl Pfeiffer), Marilyn Monroe (Peggy), J. Carroll Nash (Uncle Vince), Keith Andes (Joe Doyle)
Running Time: 105 minutes
Premiere: June 1952 (first reviewed by the *New York Times*, June 19, 1952)
16mm. Rental: Kit Parker, Audio-Brandon, and others

THE BLUE GARDENIA (Blue Gardenia Productions–Gloria Films, released by Warner Bros., 1953)
Producer: Alex Gottlieb
Screenplay: Charles Hoffmann, based on a story by Vera Caspary
Photography: Daniel Hall
Music: Raoul Kraushaar; song "Blue Gardenia" by Bob Russell and Lester Lee, arranged by Nelson Riddle (sung by Nat "King " Cole)
Editor: Edward Mann
Special Effects: Willis Cook
Script Supervisor: Don McDougal
Cast: Anne Baxter (Norah Larkin), Richard Conte (Casey Mayo), Ann Sothern (Chrystal Carpenter), Raymond Burr (Harry Prebble), Nat 'King' Cole (himself)
Running Time: 90 minutes
Premiere: March 28, 1953 (first reviewed by the *New York Times*, April 28, 1953)

THE BIG HEAT (Columbia, 1953)
Producer: Robert Arthur
Assistant Director: Milton Feldman
Screenplay: Sidney Boehm, based on the novel of the same title by William P. McGiven
Photography: Charles Lang, Jr.
Art Direction: Robert Peterson
Set Decoration: William Kiernan
Music: Daniele Amfitheatrof
Editor: Charles Nelson
Cast: Glenn Ford (Dave Bannion), Gloria Grahame (Debbie Marsh), Jocelyn Brando (Katie Bannion), Alexander Scourby (Mike Lagana), Lee Marvin (Vince Stone), Jeanette Nolan (Bertha Duncan), Peter Whitney (Tierney), Willia Bouchey (Lt. Wilkes)
Running Time: 90 minutes

Premiere: October 1953 (first reviewed by the *New York Times*, October
    15, 1953)
16mm. Rental: Budget, Audio-Brandon, and others

HUMAN DESIRE (Columbia, 1954)
Producer: Lewis J. Rachmil (Jerry Wald)
Assistant Director: Milton Feldman
Screenplay: Alfred Hayes, based on *La Bête Humaine* by Emil Zola
Photography: Burnett Cuffey
Art Direction: Robert Peterson
Set Decoration: William Kiernan
Music: Daniele Amfitheatrof
Editor: Aaron Stell
Cast: Glenn Ford (Jeff Warren), Gloria Grahame (Vicky Buckley),
    Broderick Crawford (Carl Buckley)
Running Time: 90 minutes
Premiere: September 1954 (first reviewed by the *New York Times*, August
    7, 1954)
16mm. Rental: Budget

MOONFLEET (Metro-Goldwyn-Mayer, 1955)
Producer: John Houseman
Associate Producer: Jud Kinberg
Assistant Director: Sid Sidman
Screenplay: Jan Lustig, Margaret Fitts, based on the novel of the same title
    by John Meade Falkner
Photography (Eastman Color and CinemaScope): Robert Planck
Art Direction: Cedric Gibbons, Hans Peters
Set Decoration: Edwin B. Willis, Richard Pefferle
Costumes: Walter Plunkett
Music: Miklos Rozsa; Flamenco music by Vincent Gomez
Editor: Albert Akst
Cast: Stewart Granger (Jeremy Fox), George Sanders (Lord Ashwood), Joan
    Greenwood (Lady Ashwood), Viveca Lindfors (Mrs. Minton), John
    Whiteley (John Mohune)
Running Time: 89 minutes
Premiere: June 1955 (first reviewed by the *New York Times*, June 25, 1955)
16mm. Rental: Films, Inc.

WHILE THE CITY SLEEPS (Thor Productions–RKO Teleradio Pictures,
    released by RKO Radio, 1956)
Producer: Bert E. Friedlob
Assistant Director: Ronnie Rondell

Screenplay: Casey Robinson, based on the novel *The Bloody Spur* by Charles Einstein
Photography (SuperScope): Ernest Laszlo
Art Direction: Carroll Clark
Set Decoration: Jack Mills
Costumes: Norma
Music: Herschel Burke Gilbert
Editor: Gene Fowler, Jr.
Sound Editor: Verna Fields
Cast: Dana Andrews (Edward Mobley), Rhonda Fleming (Dorothy Kyne), Sally Forest (Nancy Liggett), Thomas Mitchell (Griffith), Vincent Price (Walter Kyne, Jr.) Howard Duff (Lt. Kaufman), Ida Lupino (Mildred), George Sanders (Mark Loving), John Barrymore, Jr. (Robert Manners), Mae Marsh (Mrs. Manners)
Running Time: 100 minutes
Premiere: May 1956 (first reviewed by *New York Times*, May 17, 1956)
16mm. Rental: Kit Parker, Audio-Brandon

BEYOND A REASONABLE DOUBT (RKO Teleradio Pictures, released by RKO Radio, 1956)
Producer: Bert E. Friedlob
Assistant Director: Maxwell Henry
Screenplay: Douglas Morrow
Photography (RKO-Scope): William Snyder
Art Direction: Carroll Clark
Set Decoration: Darrell Silvera
Music: Herschel Burke Gilbert; song "Beyond a Reasonable Doubt" by Gilbert, Alfred Perry (sung by The Hi-Los)
Editor: Gene Fowler, Jr.
Cast: Dana Andrews (Tom Garret), Joan Fontaine (Susan Spencer), Sidney Blackmer (Austin Spencer), Philip Bourneuf (Thompson), Edward Binns (Lt. Kennedy)
Running Time: 80 minutes
Premiere: September 5, 1956 (first reviewed by the *New York Times*, September 14, 1956)
16mm. Rental: Kit Parker, Budget, and others

DER TIGER VON ESCHNAPUR (THE TIGER OF BENGAL)/DAS IN-DISCHE GRABMAL (THE HINDU TOMB) (A West German-French-Italian Coproduction: CCC-Films–Artur Brauner–Gloria Film–Regina Films–Critérion Films–Rizzoli Films–Impéria Films Distribution, 1959)
Executive Producer: Artur Brauner
Producers: Louise de Masure, Eberhard Meischner

Screenplay: Fritz Lang, Werner Jörg Lüddecke, based on a novel by Thea
  von Harbou and a scenario by Fritz Lang and Thea von Harbou
Photography (ColorScope): Richard Angst
Art Direction: Helmut Nentwig, Willy Schatz
Costumes: Claudia Herberg, Günther Brosda
Music: Michel Michelet *(Tiger)*, Gerhard Becker *(Grabmal)*
Choreographers: Robby Gay, Billy Daniel
Editor: Walter Wischniewsky
Cast: Debra Paget (Seeta), Paul Hubschmid (Harold Berger—Henri Mer-
  cier in French version), Walter Reyer (Chandra), Claus Holm (Dr. Wal-
  ter Rhode), Sabine Bethmann (Irene Rhode)
Running Time: *(Tiger)* 95 minutes, *(Grabmal)* 101 minutes
Premiere: March 5, 1959, Universum, Stuttgart
American Premiere: In a single 95-minute film called *Journey to the Lost
  City*, October 1960 (first reviewed by the *New York Times*, December 8,
  1960)
16mm. Rental: National Film Service

**DIE TAUSEND AUGEN DES DR. MABUSE (THE THOUSAND EYES
OF DR. MABUSE)** (A West German-French-Italian Coproduction: CCC
  Filmkunst–Critérion Films–Cei-Incom-Omnia Distribution, 1960)
Producer: Fritz Lang
Executive Producer: Artur Brauner
Screenplay: Fritz Lang, Heinz Oskar Wuttig, based on an idea of Jan
  Fethke and the character created by Norbert Jacques
Photography: Karl Loeb
Art Direction: Erich Kettlehut, Johannes Ott
Costumes: Ina Stein
Music: Bert Grund
Editors: Walter and Waltraute Wischniewsky
Cast: Dawn Addams (Marion Menil), Peter Van Eyck (Henry B. Travers),
  Wolfgang Preiss (Jordan), Lupo Prezzo (Cornelius), Gert Fröbe (Com-
  missioner Kraus), Werner Peters (Hieronymous P. Mistelzweig)
Running Time: 103 minutes
Premiere: May 14, 1960, Gloria-Palast, Stuttgart
American Premiere: 1966
16mm. Rental: Budget, Audio-Brandon, and others

Index

197